Federalism:
An Introduction

Federalism: An Introduction

George Anderson
Forum of Federations

OXFORD
UNIVERSITY PRESS

OXFORD
UNIVERSITY PRESS
70 Wynford Drive, Don Mills, Ontario M3C 1J9
www.oup.com/ca

Oxford University Press is a department of the University of Oxford. It
furthers the University's objective of excellence in research, scholarship, and
education by publishing worldwide in
Oxford   New York
Auckland   Cape Town   Dar es Salaam   Hong Kong   Karachi
Kuala Lumpur   Madrid   Melbourne   Mexico City   Nairobi
New Delhi   Shanghai   Taipei   Toronto

With offices in
Argentina   Austria   Brazil   Chile   Czech Republic   France   Greece
Guatemala   Hungary   Italy   Japan   Poland   Portugal   Singapore
South Korea   Switzerland   Thailand   Turkey   Ukraine   Vietnam

Oxford is a trade mark of Oxford University Press
in the UK and in certain other countries

Published in Canada by Oxford University Press
Copyright © 2008 Forum of Federations

The moral rights of the author have been asserted

Database right Oxford University Press (maker)

Library and Archives Canada Cataloguing in Publication

Anderson, George, 1945-
Federalism : an introduction / George Anderson.

Includes bibliographical references and index.
ISBN 978-0-19-542904-6

1. Federal government—Textbooks. I. Title.
JC355.A54 2008   321.02   C2007-905545-1

Printed in India.
1 2 3 4 — 11 10 09 08

This is an authorized advance edition of *Federalism: An Introduction*,
to be published in February 2008 by Oxford University Press.

Table of Contents

Preface

This introduction to federalism has been written primarily for practitioners of government—politicians, government officials, journalists, members of non-governmental and international organizations and concerned citizens—who have a practical interest in federalism, probably focused on federalism in their own or other specific countries. They might ask, 'What can I learn from the experience of other federal countries that might help me better understand the nature, choices, and even limitations that this country might face in modifying or developing its form of federalism?' At the same time, it is hoped that students of federalism find the book a useful, concise overview.

The book's language is simple, with a minimum of jargon, no footnotes, and no references to particular authors. It gives the essential points in a direct, bottom-line way useful to people engaged in political debate or policy making.

There can be no one recipe for federalism. Every society is complex and its character is shaped by many factors. Thus, this book is less about 'how to do' and more about 'what to consider'. It outlines what factors might be relevant and gives a sense of how they might play out. The catalogue of factors can never be complete and some factors could play out quite differently, depending on context. So the information provided here needs to be joined with a good knowledge of the country of particular interest. Even so, sophisticated constitutional authors have sometimes been surprised at how their designs have worked in practice.

The book falls into 10 chapters, which are divided into sections, each of which starts with a brief statement in bold type that outlines the key points of the section. It is possible to get a quick overview of the whole book simply by reading these short statements. Elaboration follows that further develops the ideas and introduces additional material. As well, there are boxes with examples of the experience of different federations in relation to a particular aspect of federalism. The boxes are illustrative, not comprehensive: they provide a sense of the range of possibilities. They can be skipped or read at choice. It is hoped this way of presenting the material promotes flexible use, facilitates understanding, and responds to the different needs of readers. This is an introduction and many readers will wish to deepen their knowledge. If the book inspires further reading, so much the better: a brief list of suggestions is provided at the end of the text.

The Forum of Federations is active on six continents and envisages making extensive use of this book, which I wrote to respond to a need we saw for a concise, non-academic overview of federalism. We would be grateful for any suggestions to improve subsequent editions.

George Anderson,
President and CEO,
Forum of Federations

Chapter One

An Overview of Federalism

Federalism's importance

Federalism is increasingly important in the world.

- Twenty-eight countries, home to over 40 per cent of the world's people, either call themselves federal or are generally considered to be federal.

- Almost all democracies with very large areas or very large populations are federal.

- With democratization, Argentina, Brazil, and Mexico are becoming increasingly federal.

- Belgium, Ethiopia, and Spain are formerly unitary countries that have become federal.

- Federalism has been adopted in post-conflict environments in Bosnia, the Democratic Republic of Congo, Iraq, Sudan, and South Africa, and is being considered in Sri Lanka and Nepal.

- The European Union has a number of federal characteristics.

The World's Federations

Argentina, Australia, Austria, Belau, Belgium, Bosnia-Herzegovina, Brazil, Canada, Comoros, Democratic Republic of Congo*, Ethiopia, Germany, India, Iraq*, Malaysia, Mexico, Micronesia, Nigeria, Pakistan, Russia, St. Kitts and Nevis, South Africa, Spain, Sudan*, Switzerland, United Arab Emirates, United States of America, Venezuela

*Post-conflict societies whose federal constitutions are not consolidated

---

Federalism's variety

Federalism comes in many varieties and contexts

Federations differ greatly in their social and economic composition and their institutions. They include very large and very small countries, rich and poor countries, countries that have very homogenous and very diverse populations. Some federations are long-standing democracies, while others have more recent and troubled histories of democracy.

Federal structures—the internal institutional arrangements—vary greatly. Federations can have as few as two territorial units or more than 80. Some federations are highly centralized, concentrating power in the central government*, while others are decentralized, with extensive autonomy and discretion allocated to constituent units. Some have quite clear divisions of powers between the central and the territorial governments, while others have widely overlapping powers. Some have prime ministers and parliamentary governments; others have presidents and congressional institutions. They may have proportional representation or plurality electoral laws. They may have only two political parties, or several. Some federations are stable and harmonious, while others are unstable and divided. All of these factors affect the functioning and success of different federal regimes. No one model would be appropriate in all circumstances. The capacity for variety is one of federalism's strengths.

Federalism's common characteristics

Despite many differences, a few common characteristics distinguish federal systems from other kinds of government.

The following characteristics are usually thought to make a system of government federal:

- **At least two orders of government,** one for the whole country and the other for the regions. Each government has a direct electoral relationship with its citizens. The regions have many names: we shall refer to them as the 'constituent units' of the federation.

Examples of the Names of Constituent Units

The most common names of constituent units are *states* (**Australia, Brazil, Ethiopia, India, Malaysia, Mexico, Nigeria, and the US**) and *provinces* (**Argentina, Canada, Pakistan, South Africa**). But other terms are *Länder* (**Austria and Germany**) and *cantons* (**Switzerland**). There are both regions and communities in Belgium and autonomous communities in Spain. Russia has regions, republics, autonomous areas, territories, and cities of federal significance. Some small federations have islands.

- **A written constitution** some parts of which cannot be amended by the federal government alone. Major amendments affecting the constituent units commonly require substantial consent from them as well as from the central government.

- A constitution that formally allocates legislative, including fiscal, powers to the two orders of government ensuring **some genuine autonomy for each order.** However, federations differ greatly in the way and extent to which they define distinct powers for the two orders.

- Usually some special arrangements, notably in **upper houses,** for the representation of the constituent units in key central institutions to provide for regional input in central decision-making, often with greater weight given to smaller units than their population would otherwise merit.

- An umpire or procedure (usually involving **courts**, but sometimes referendums or an upper house) to rule on constitutional disputes between governments.

- A set of processes and institutions for facilitating or conducting **relations between governments**.

If there is an **essence of federalism**, it is that there are **two constitutionally established orders of government with some genuine autonomy from each other, and the governments at each level are primarily accountable to their respective electorates.**

The more specific design features of each federation reflect local institutional traditions, and the desired level and kind of autonomy sought. Normally, federalism requires democracy and the rule of law because non-democratic regimes usually do not permit genuine autonomy for constituent units.

Not all of the 28 countries listed on page nine fully meet all the criteria for federalism. Some are very centralized and weakly federal. Others have special unitary features that may sometimes permit the central government to override the autonomy of constituent units. Does this mean they are not federal? There is no definitive answer. As a practical matter, the issue is whether the country normally operates in a federal manner; i.e., that there is some genuine, constitutionally based autonomy at both levels.

Finally, in some countries the word 'federal' is avoided because of historic or symbolic political connotations. Thus most experts would say Spain and South Africa are federal, but many in those countries resist the term because they associate it, respectively, with undermining national unity or with the Apartheid regime. Indonesia rejected the federalism the Dutch tried to impose before independence and is unlikely to use the term even as it becomes more federal in practice.

Federalism and devolved government

In confederal systems, the central government is a legal creation of the constituent units. In unitary systems, any regional governments are legal creations of the central institutions. In federal systems, each order of government has an autonomous constitutional existence. Some unitary countries are more decentralized in practice than some federations.

The two oldest federations, the United States and Switzerland, started as confederations. Typically these regimes proved weak and unstable. It is debatable whether there are any real confederations in the modern world. The European Union is a unique political creation with both confederal and federal features. Benelux is a confederal arrangement of a limited kind, as it CARICOM in the Caribbean. The United Arab Emirates calls itself a federation, but has many confederal features.

Most countries have a unitary system of government. Often they have regional administrative structures with no elected government. In other cases, they can have constituent units (often called provinces or regions) with independently elected governments and substantial responsibilities, but such governments derive all their powers from the central government or legislature, which could, in principle, take them back. However, in many cases it is hard to imagine such a political reversal, so some unitary countries can have strong similarities to federations. In fact, some unitary countries have devolved more substantial powers to their constituent units than have some federations. So federations are usually, but not always, more decentralized in practice than unitary regimes.

Devolved Unitary Regimes

Some unitary countries, such as **Columbia**, **Italy**, and **Japan**, have relatively strong regional governments. Many formerly centralized unitary regimes, such as **France** and **Peru**, are moving towards significant devolution to elected regional governments. In some cases, there are strong political pressures from particular regions for devolution: thus, the **United Kingdom** has devolved substantial powers to the Scottish Parliament, notably over education, health, and local affairs (and lesser powers to Wales and Northern Ireland). **Indonesia** has recently moved to transfer many responsibilities to provinces and localities, with special arrangements for Aceh. Much of the analysis in this primer would apply to such countries. Some may become fully federal.

Chapter Two

Choosing Federalism

Origins of federations

Federations have arisen in very different circumstances, each being the unique result of choices by political leaders and larger historical forces. Federalism has been chosen to bring together formerly separate units into a new country, or to rearrange a previously unitary country, and even as a product of both processes together.

Every federation is unique. Few generalizations can safely be made about how and why federations are created and evolve. However, in every case of federalization, political leaders have constitutionalized two tiers of government as a way to realize and reconcile their respective goals while minimizing violence—or in some cases in order to end it.

Today there are 192 countries in the United Nations, and approximately 28 are federal. Most countries did not exist within their current boundaries a century ago and only a handful did so two centuries ago. Each country has its own story regarding its origins and its territorial and political evolution. These stories involve wars and revolutions, dynastic marriages, colonial empires, international treaties, and peaceful democratic processes.

Federations have emerged within these larger processes of country formation and evolution in a variety of ways:

• In some cases, **coming together** was central to the emergence of a new, federal country. Previously separate units—independent states or colonies—concluded that they had enough common interest and shared identity to join together in a federal arrangement. Why federal? Because a federal structure permitted each unit to preserve some of its autonomy while pooling other aspects in the new community.

- In other cases, the country may have originally been created with a unitary and highly centralized (often authoritarian and undemocratic) structure. The eventual choice of federalism was in response to democratic political pressures for **devolution** because of the country's multiple languages, religions or ethnicities, and, perhaps, major economic differences between regions. In some countries, the regions pressing for autonomy may have been distinct political entities in the past.

- In yet other cases, these two processes combined. Canada emerged from the creation of Ontario and Quebec out of a previously unitary regime and from the addition of new provinces. India too combined these two processes.

Historic waves of federalism

Federations have been formed in a series of historical waves over the last two centuries.

The first wave, from the late eighteenth to the early twentieth centuries, saw the **creation of new countries with formerly independent units coming together in a federal form**. Switzerland and the United States initially came together as confederations: the American experiment with confederation lasted for only eight years, from 1781 to 1789, when the 13 states addressed a weakness at the centre by forming the first modern federation; the Swiss confederation evolved over more than five centuries, but after a brief civil war it adopted, in 1848, a federal constitution modeled on the American example. Germany's first federal constitution emerged in 1871 as a successor to loose confederal arrangements. While Canada was initially formed in 1867 out of the coming together of three colonies in British North America (and in due course expanded by the addition of others), its federal bargain included splitting the largest of these into two provinces—so its origins were both in coming together and devolution. The six colonies in Australia came together as a federation in 1901.

In Latin America, four federations emerged in the nineteenth and early twentieth centuries. They all won independence following Napoleon's conquest of Spain, but then had checkered constitutional histories with periods of dictatorship and civil unrest. Their federal constitutions emerged over time, sometimes after earlier experiments with both federal and unitary regimes. In the last 20 years, the transition to genuine democracy in Argentina, Brazil and Mexico has brought real life to their federal constitutional arrangements. Venezuela is now highly centralized.

The post-war break-up of the European empires saw the creation of various **post-colonial federations**, as well as some failed attempts. India, Pakistan, Malaysia, and Nigeria have endured as federal systems. The efforts by the departing colonial powers to bring together formerly separate colonies into new federal countries were not a success in the West Indies, Central Africa, French West Africa, and East Africa, nor were attempts to introduce federal arrangements in Indonesia, Mali, and Uganda. The very small federations of Belau, Comoros, Micronesia, and St. Kitts and Nevis did emerge from decolonization.

The next significant wave came with **new federations emerging from the collapse of communism**. The communist Soviet Union, Czechoslovakia, and Yugoslavia all had nominally federal constitutions, but were in reality centrally controlled one-party regimes. However, as they democratized, their federal structures took on real political significance. With little experience of democracy and the tremendous stresses of transition, all these federations failed. However, Russia, which itself had been a federation within the old structures of the Soviet Union, did emerge as a post-communist federation. And Bosnia-Hersegovina emerged out of Yugoslavia with a federal structure, though it remains under a strong measure of international tutelage.

About the same time, **new federations were emerging from unitary states**. Belgium is the clearest example, formally adopting a federal constitution in 1993. As Spain democratized after Franco, it devolved significant powers to its autonomous regions and became effectively federal. South Africa also adopted an essentially federal structure (along German lines), when it democratized after the end of apartheid. Other countries—Italy, Indonesia, Peru, UK—moved towards substantial devolution to regional governments, but they are not yet fully federal. Both Bolivia and the Philippines have debated adopting federalism.

The most difficult cases have been the **new federations emerging from post-conflict situations**. Under the Dayton Accord, Bosnia-Herzegovina was established as a federal regime; however, it has remained under a kind of international supervision. Ethiopia, which had never been democratic, adopted federalism after rebels defeated the Mengistu regime, as did Sudan as part of a comprehensive peace accord that ended its long civil war with the South. The Congo's new constitution, under which it recently conducted the first nation-wide elections, is effectively federal. Iraq's voters ratified a federal constitution in 2005, but its implementation is proving to be very challenging. All of these situations remain difficult. In other cases, such as Sri Lanka and Cyprus, efforts to find a federal formula to end conflict and division have failed so far. Nepal is currently looking at the possibility of federalism, following the end of its civil war.

The last case that should be mentioned in the history of federalism is the European Union. The EU is a unique political institution, perhaps more confederal than federal, but it has a number of federal features, and there is a continuing debate amongst Europeans about whether to move more fully in a federal direction. In any case, the EU experiment remains highly relevant for students of federalism.

Evolution of federations

All federations evolve over time. Some have gone through major formal constitutional changes, while others have changed significantly despite largely stable constitutions. Factors such as the creation of new constituent units, urbanization, major demographic and economic shifts, new technologies, major global and domestic political developments, and the experience of democracy have been critical in shaping federal experiences.

The oldest federation, the United States, has had the same constitution for over 200 years and has made only 27 amendments to it. India has made 94 amendments to its constitution in 60 years. Brazil has had seven constitutions since independence, Mexico six, and Venezuela 26. Some federations have maintained constitutional continuity, while others have had legal breaks because of revolutions or military regimes. As will be noted, in many federations the number and character of constituent units have changed dramatically over time. Whatever the extent of formal constitutional changes, every federation has changed over time, often in ways that would have surprised the founders. The United States and Australia were to be decentralized federations, but have become centralized, while Canada, which was to be centralized, evolved in the opposite direction.

In all long-established federations, transportation and communications technologies have shrunk distances and shaped the development of politically conscious communities within them. As well, parts of a country that in the early history of the federation may not have existed or have counted for little—the west of the United States and Canada, the interior and north of Brazil—have assumed greater weight over time. The world wars, which called for major national efforts, greatly strengthened some central governments in federations, as has the rise of the welfare state.

The experience of democracy has been critically important in the changing shape of many federations. Mexico and Brazil have become more federal as democracy has shifted power to multiple centres and parties. India has defied skeptics and maintained the world's largest democracy, but it functions very differently today than in the period after independence when the Congress party controlled both the Union and all the state governments.

Suitability of federalism

Federalism is not always best, and there is no best version of federalism. Federalism seems particularly suited to democracies with very large populations or territories or with highly diverse populations that are regionally concentrated. Over time, federalism requires a significant part of the population to have a sense of identity with the whole country, as well as lively and engaged political communities at the regional level.

Federalism is suitable for some countries, not all. Federalism is a democratic form of government, rooted in constitutionalism and the rule of law. It can be a sham in non-democratic countries, though there have been cases of partial democracy or liberalization where federal structures had some real life.

Federalism and Democracy

The **Soviet Union**, **Yugoslavia** and **Czechoslovakia** were not true federations during the period of Communist rule, even though they had federal constitutions. All real power was centralized in the Communist Party. The situation was more complex in Latin America: **Brazil** and **Argentina** had periods of military rule at the centre, but sometimes allowed relatively free elections within their states or provinces (particularly during transition from military rule; in Brazil, the states played a key role in designing the constitution to end such rule). In **Mexico**, the Institutional Revolutionary Party (PRI) largely controlled elections for many years, but over time its grip loosened, particularly in certain states. **Nigeria** and **Pakistan** have had similar experiences of intermittent military rule and federal democracy. Thus, some undemocratic federations are clearly for show, but in others their federal structure might have some reality. Moreover, in all these countries, federal constitutional arrangements came to have real significance during the transition to democracy as previously subservient constituent units were empowered. In the formerly communist countries, the federal structure played a role in their break-up.

It is no accident that all democracies with populations much larger than 100 million people are federal (Japan and Indonesia are the largest non-federal democracies, but both are regionalized) and all continental-sized democracies are federal. There seems to be a limit to the size of population or territory that a single, popularly elected government can manage effectively. As well, highly diverse democracies, especially those with distinct, regionally concentrated populations, typically have pressures to give these populations their own governments for certain purposes. Thus federalism is increasingly proving to be attractive to some formerly unitary countries, as well as to developing or transitional countries that are seeking a viable form of democracy.

Of course, federal democracies, like unitary democracies, require certain cultural and other characteristics, including respect for the rule of law and minority rights and an element of shared identity. Judgments can be wrong about where democracy can survive. There are many more democracies today than twenty or forty years ago. Sixty years ago, many doubted that India could hold together as a peaceful democracy, but it has. Moreover, India's success in surviving as a democracy was actually dependent on its adopting federalism.

However, a number of federations have failed, especially early in their existence. Most had had little experience of democracy, little history as a shared country, and a weak sense of common identity. The post-communist and some post-colonial federations failed because of the stresses of democracy as well as other factors, such as extreme imbalance of constituent units or fatally weak central governments. Local or regional identities were stronger than any larger national identity and were seen as inconsistent with or opposed to such an identity. Failure took the form of break-up or secession (or even expulsion in the case of Singapore's leaving Malaysia).

Chapter Three

The Constituent Units

The political geometry of federations

Federations are shaped by their political geometry. They can have as few as two constituent units or over 80. The one or two largest units may constitute a clear majority of the country or have only a small relative weight. The largest units can be much bigger than the smallest ones or relatively close in size. Very small or less developed units may lack the capacity to take on some governmental responsibilities.

The population of federations varies from well over a billion people in India to only 46,000 in St. Kitts and Nevis. The largest constituent unit in some federations is bigger than many countries: Uttar Pradesh in India has 160 million people, while California has 34 million. At the other extreme, there are some tiny constituent units (excluding special units): Nevis has only 12,000 people, but, even in a large federation such as Russia, the Evenki autonomous area has only 14,000 people. Obviously, these questions of absolute size affect governmental capacity and political dynamics.

The number and relative sizes of constituent units help shape a federation's politics. Russia and the United States have the largest number of units—86 and 50 respectively—and the largest units constitute a relatively small portion of the national population (Moscow, seven per cent; California, 12 per cent). Having so many units, none of which is relatively very large, may have facilitated the centralization of powers in these countries. Since its return to civilian rule, the same could be said of Nigeria, with 36 states, none of which is more than seven per cent of the population.

At the other extreme, federations with two to four units typically have one dominant region and quite unstable politics, often including a separatist movement, though it varies whether the larger or a smaller region is separatist.

Federations with Very Few Constituent Units

St. Kitts and Nevis consists of two islands, with 75 per cent of the population in St. Kitts. **Bosnia-Herzegovina** has two entities, with the Bosniac-Croat Federation constituting 61 per cent of the population. Of the **Comoros'** three islands, Grande Comoros has 51 per cent of the population. **Micronesia** has four states, with 50 per cent of the population in Chuuk. **Belgium's** three regions also have three cultural communities), with 58 per cent of the population base in Flanders. Modern **Pakistan** has four provinces, with 56 per cent of the population in Punjab; the original Pakistan had only two provinces, East and West (separated by India), from which Bangladesh seceded after a brief civil war in 1971. **Czechoslovakia** emerged from Communist rule as a dual Czech-Slovak federation, but failed within three years. **Nigeria** originally had only three regions, with the North accounting for over 50 per cent of the population. The country's early history was marked by constant interregional tensions, which culminated in the breakdown of civilian government and a tragic civil war. Nigeria now has 36 states. In all of these cases, the small number of units and the fact of half or more of the population being in one unit have created tensions and instability. Dual federations are particularly prey to demands by the smaller unit for equality in central decision making, which the larger unit often resists.

Most federations fall between these extremes and have from six (Australia) to 31 (Mexico) constituent units. Such numbers seem to make intergovernmental relations more manageable and the systems relatively stable (though it is striking how much the European

Community has focused on its decision-making regime as it has grown from six to twenty-seven member states). A few of these federations have a particularly populous unit (Ontario has 39 per cent of Canada's population; Buenos Aires province, 38 per cent of Argentina's; New South Wales, 34 per cent of Australia's), which can play a central role in the country's politics and create tensions with other parts of the country. Of course, other factors affect tensions within federations as well, notably their internal diversity.

Types of constituent units

Federations are typically made up of one principal category of constituent unit, often called a state or province, at the subnational level. Frequently, there are secondary classes as well—notably for less developed territories and capital regions. Territories have often acquired the status of full constituent units over time. Some federations have constitutionalized municipal government as a third tier.

Federations typically divide their territory into one main class of constituent unit, such as states or provinces. However, some federations have special territorial units with lesser constitutional status, usually making them legally subject to the central government. These might be the national capital district, remote and thinly populated territories, special tribal areas, or overseas possessions. They may also have special funding arrangements. With the exception of the national capital districts, such special territorial units usually have a relatively small population, with little weight in the functioning of the federation. Some federations, notably those populated largely by immigrants, have created new constituent units out of territories as they have become more populous and developed. (The issue of admitting new states into the Union was a central cause of the American Civil War.)

Territories in Federal Systems

The **United States** grew from 13 states to 50, largely through the addition of new territories out of which states were created. **Canada** created two new provinces out of former territories and substantially enlarged four others. **Brazil** has created new states out of territories, as recently as 1988. Today, Canada has three existing territories, Australia one, and India seven union territories, all of which have a very small population within the national context.

Argentina, Australia, Belgium, Brazil, Ethiopia, Mexico, Nigeria, and the United States have arrangements whereby their national capital territory or district is not part of a normal constituent unit.

Russia has a complex variety of constituent units—republics, regions (*oblasts*), territories (*krais*), autonomous areas (*okrugs*), and cities of federal significance—but under the Putin regime their status or powers ceased to differ significantly.

In most federations, the definition and powers of municipal and local government are within the legal jurisdiction of the constituent-unit governments. Some federations (Brazil, India, Mexico, South Africa) have constitutionalized this tier of government, thus giving it some independent status, though less than that of the constituent units at the state or provincial level.

The social diversity of constituent units

Federations vary greatly in how much the composition of constituent units reflects regionally distinct populations.

Some federations—Argentina, Austria, Australia, Brazil, Germany, Mexico, the United States—have a clearly dominant language and relatively low levels of religious or ethnic division. They can have important regional differences, but the definition of their federal units has not been structured around managing ethnic, religious, or linguistic cleavages. In highly diverse federations, citizens can feel distinct identities strongly, and cleavages around these are typically a central feature of political life. When such groups are regionally concentrated, the character and composition of the constituent units can be a critical aspect of the federal system.

Reflecting Diversity in the Composition of Constituent Units

Switzerland, with three major languages, two religions and a mountainous countryside, is divided into 20 full cantons and six half-cantons, most of which are unilingual and have a clearly predominant Protestant or Catholic majority. **India** originally resisted defining its states on the basis of ethnicity and language, fearing it would heighten divisions; but, between 1956 and 1966, state boundaries were redrawn along these lines, with one state (Punjab) having a distinctive religious dimension as well. **Canada's** French-speaking population is heavily concentrated in Quebec, while the other nine provinces have English-speaking majorities. **Ethiopia's** new federation was explicitly established along ethnic lines, but some states still have very diverse composition, which creates pressures. Spain's move to federalism has permitted the re-emergence of historic nationalities as political units. **Belgium** is unique in having two-tier federalism to reflect both territorial and cultural divisions: however, the territorial divisions also reflect linguistic differences, except for Brussels. **Nigeria's** 36 states are largely defined in accord with major linguistic, ethnic, and religious divisions. **Russia's** predominant ethnicity and language is Russian, but many of its smaller constituent units have a distinct ethnic or linguistic majority.

Some federations have a clear linguistic or ethnic majority (Belgium, Canada, Spain, and Russia), but with one large minority (Belgium and Canada) or several smaller minorities (Spain and Russia), while others (Ethiopia, India, Nigeria) have an exceptional number of languages, religions, and nationalities, with none constituting a national majority. Often ethnic, linguistic and religious cleavages cut across one another—Switzerland is the classic case—and this can help reduce social polarization. It is often harder for a society to manage one dominant cleavage or strongly reinforcing cleavages between two very distinct populations than it is to deal with a number of cleavages across several populations.

Federalism can be helpful in accommodating such diversity, in that important, regionally concentrated populations can be majorities in their respective constituent units. However, not all groups are large enough or concentrated enough to fit a constituent unit and no territorially defined unit ever has a perfectly homogenous population. So the rights of minorities within the units and demands for new constituent units for these 'minorities within minorities' must be considered. As well, in some countries, there are secessionist pressures that can be affected by the nature of constituent units (as is discussed further in chapter nine). The political importance of differences, whether of religion or language or ethnicity, depends on strength of identity and attitudes: there are cases where once politically divisive differences, such as between Protestants and Catholics, remain statistically important, but have lost their political significance over time.

Establishing and changing boundaries

It is typically difficult to reduce the territory of existing constituent units in federations once they are established. Creating new units or expanding them out of territorial lands is easier. Redefinition of boundaries has sometimes happened in exceptional periods of civil war or military rule. Unitary countries that federalize may follow historic boundaries or need to develop new criteria for drawing boundaries.

While the number and character of a federation's constituent units can strongly affect its functioning and stability, it is normally very difficult to reduce the territory of established constituent units during normal periods of democratic government. Often the constituent units must agree themselves, usually through a procedure involving a referendum. The most dramatic cases have been in India, where the states have no say, and in Nigeria, where military regimes have redrawn boundaries extensively.

A more usual democratic procedure has been the creation of new states and provinces out of the former territories of the US, Brazil, Argentina, and Canada. Most federations have special amending procedures for creating new constituent units, often requiring some measure of consent from existing constituent units or at least a special majority in the upper house.

Redrawing Boundaries of Existing Constituent Units

India's central Parliament decided in the mid-1950s to systematically redraw state boundaries, typically to reflect major linguistic differences; it had the constitutional power to do this without state consent. **Nigeria** has gone from three states at independence to 36 ethnically based states today, almost always by fiat of military regimes when democracy was suspended. **Switzerland** created the new canton of Jura after a complicated referendum procedure. **Russia** has amalgamated 11 units into five following referendums. **Germany** amalgamated two *Länder* shortly after creating its new federation. **Canada** substantially enlarged certain provinces by adding former 'territorial' lands to them. In the **United States**, West Virginia was created when Virginia split during the civil war.

Formerly unitary countries must decide the number and boundaries of units if they become federal. The boundaries of new units may follow traditional boundaries of administrative units or former political units (as in Spain). In some cases, the division can be based on census data regarding the characteristics of the local population or on a referendum. The issue of the number of units and their boundaries can be particularly challenging in federalizing a country with no tradition of significant internal units or boundaries: this is a central issue in Iraq and in Nepal's debate over federalism.

Chapter Four

Dividing Powers — Who Does What and How?

Two models for assigning legal powers

There are two broadly different approaches to distributing powers within federations: the dualist and integrated models. Many countries have elements of both. The dualist model typically assigns different jurisdictions to each order of government, which then delivers and administers its own programs. The integrated model provides for many shared competences and the constituent-unit governments often administer centrally legislated programs or laws.

Under the dualist, or classical, model of federalism, constitutional jurisdiction over different subjects is usually assigned exclusively to one order of government. In this model, each order of government normally delivers programs in its area of responsibility, using its civil service and departments; the federal government's departments are thus present throughout the country.

In practice, the dualist model does not achieve a neat separation of powers because so many issues have regional, national, and even international dimensions and many different responsibilities of governments are themselves intertwined.

- In all dualist constitutions there are some shared or **concurrent powers** in which both orders of government can make laws. Canada and Belgium have few concurrent powers, while Australia has very extensive concurrency. Where powers are concurrent, federal law is generally, but not always, paramount, meaning it prevails in cases of conflict.

- In addition, there can be **de facto concurrency** when both orders of government have different powers that bear on a question: this is **a kind of shared power** and typically it does not involve paramountcy. For example, in old constitutions, the environment is not usually a head of power, but both orders of government may have different legal powers that permit them to regulate the environmental impacts of a major infrastructure project, so it can proceed only if they both agree

Under the integrated (or interlocking) model of federalism, exemplified by Germany, some subject matters are exclusively assigned to one order of government (e.g., defence to the federal government), but most subject matters are concurrent, where the central government sets framework legislation that the constituent units can complement (but not contravene) with their own legislation. As well, the governments of the constituent units deliver programs in these concurrent areas. Thus the central government has a small civil service in the regions, largely limited to its areas of exclusive competence. This model is also sometimes called administrative federalism because the principal powers of the constituent units are administrative. A great challenge in this model is restricting the detail of central policy making so as to leave room for decisions and laws at the level of constituent units. The German model also provides for joint decision making in these areas of concurrency, in that federal laws must be approved by a majority vote of the representatives of the *Länder* in the Bundesrat; South Africa has adopted aspects of this model.

Canada, Brazil, and the United States are examples of largely dualist federations; Germany, Austria, South Africa, and Spain follow the interlocking model. India and Switzerland have strong features of both. Australia is largely dualist in administrative arrangements, but has so many areas of concurrency that it has some strongly interlocking features. No federation is purely of one form.

These considerations of legal powers need to be combined with the financial arrangements in a federation. The next chapter will show that the control and distribution of revenues is central to the real distribution of powers in federation.

Legal sources of powers

Normally, the distribution of legislative and fiscal powers is set out in the constitution. In some federations, the powers of individual constituent-unit governments can be substantially determined through bilateral agreements with the federal government. Some federations permit the delegation of legislative responsibility between orders of government while others do not.

All federations have provisions in their constitution dealing with the allocation of powers between the central and constituent-unit governments. Constitutions differ enormously in the level of detail and approach. For example, the United States Constitution has only 18 headings for the powers of the federal government and most of these are actually concurrent with federal paramountcy; all other powers (residual powers) lie with the states. The Indian Constitution, by contrast, has three long lists: the union list has 97 headings, the concurrent list, 47, and the state list, 66. The Spanish Constitution lists competences that may be assigned to the autonomous communities, but this is done legally through statutes of autonomy for each community, and these statutes can vary.

In many federations, interpretations by the courts and evolving practice has shifted the real division of powers significantly away from the intent of the constitution's drafters, making the federation more or less centralized than was first envisaged. This is probably most true of the older, less detailed constitutions.

Varied federal distributions of powers

While there are important commonalities between federations regarding which powers are allocated to which order of government, there are also significant differences.

Federal constitutions have been written over the last 230 years in widely different contexts. More recent constitutions reflect lessons from the experiences, good and bad, of earlier constitutions. It is not surprising, therefore, that there is great variation in the approaches taken to the distribution of powers among federations. A few powers are almost always assigned to the federal government and others almost always to the constituent-unit governments, but, for many powers, we have a pattern of tendencies, strong or weak, frequently with outliers. Sometimes there is no clear pattern. The box below gives a rough sense of these patterns. In practice, the precise allocation of powers within any federation is a complex matter that reflects not just the text of the constitution, but also court decisions and other developments.

Patterns in the Distribution of Some Powers within Federations

The following indicates tendencies regarding the allocations of powers across most federations. 'Concurrent' means both orders can make laws in a defined area, usually with federal paramouncty. 'Joint' means the two orders make some concurrent decisions together. 'Shared' means each order has some different legal powers in the broad area and decisions are made independently.

- Currency: always federal

- Defence: always federal, sometimes constituent-unit (CU)

- Treaty implementation: almost always federal, sometimes CU

- External trade: usually federal, occasionally concurrent, joint or shared

- Interstate trade: usually federal, occasionally concurrent, joint or shared

- Intrastate trade: usually CU, sometimes concurrent

- Major physical infrastructure: usually federal, sometimes concurrent, joint or shared or CU

- Primary/Secondary education: usually CU, occasionally concurrent, rarely federal

- Post-secondary education and research: no clear pattern

- Income security: mix of federal, concurrent, joint, and shared

- Pensions: either concurrent, joint, shared, or federal

- Health care: usually CU, sometimes concurrent, joint, or shared

- Mineral resources: no clear pattern

- Agriculture: no clear pattern

- Environment: usually concurrent or joint, rarely CU

- Municipal affairs*: usually CU, occasionally joint or shared

- Court system*: usually joint or concurrent, occasionally federal, rarely CU

- Criminal law: no clear pattern

- Police: usually shared, occasionally concurrent or joint, rarely federal or CU

- Customs/excise taxes: almost always federal, sometimes concurrent

- Corporate and personal taxes: usually joint, shared or concurrent, sometimes federal

* Supreme and Constitutional courts are almost always established in the constitution and are thus not a head of power. In some federations, municipal, or local governments are also constitutionally established, though the federal or CU governments may have some powers over them.

Constitutions differ not just in the assignment of powers, but also in their specificity. Even the most complete listing can overlook something, so constitutions must assign residual powers specifying which order of government gets any power that is not mentioned. Typically, residual powers go to the federal government in federations that emerged from previously unitary regimes and to the constituent-unit governments in federations that brought previously separate units together. Residual-power clauses can be important, notably in constitutions such as that of the US, where the federal powers are defined (in a short list) and residual powers are the sole source of constituent-unit powers. However, courts have tended to give broad interpretations to specified powers, whether federal or constituent unit, so the effect of residual power clauses has been less than envisaged by constitutional drafters.

Criteria for distributing powers

There is no simple formula for determining the appropriate allocation of powers between orders of government.

While there are some patterns in the allocations of powers within federations, there is also great variety. The European Union has a continuing debate on which powers to allocate to Brussels or to leave with the member states. In this regard, Europeans have developed the concept of subsidiarity, a principle that the central government should take on powers only when it is necessary to achieve an objective and when it adds value in comparison to what the governments of the constituent units could achieve on their own. While helpful, the principle has proven elusive in practice. It is notable that the European Union has not empowered Brussels in the areas of defence and foreign policy, which are the classic central powers of federations. Inevitably, each country has its own debates around the allocation of powers. Decisions will reflect questions of efficiency and effectiveness, but also, critically, views of what are shared objectives across the federation.

Asymmetry in the distribution of powers

Federations usually allocate the same powers to all of the constituent-unit governments. However, in some federations, some constituent units receive more powers than others. Constitutional asymmetry is usually limited because major asymmetry poses challenges in the management of a federation. There can also be more pragmatic forms of asymmetry.

The term 'asymmetry' is applied to many aspects of difference between the constituent units of federations: asymmetrical political weight, asymmetrical group or language rights and status, and asymmetrical powers. Each of these poses different issues. Clearly, different constituent units have different political weights because of their population, wealth, or strategic position; some federations try to limit this by giving extra weight to the representation of smaller units within central institutions. Special and distinct provisions regarding group, linguistic, or religious rights within particular constituent units are a frequent feature in very diverse federations.

Asymmetrical distributions of power between constituent units in a federation are unusual. This is particularly true of constitutionally established asymmetries. Flexibility of this kind can address demands coming from a particular region for a decentralization of a power or powers that the constituent units elsewhere may not consider a priority. However, special treatment for one constituent unit can create pressure for the same treatment for the others. As well, if the powers that are devolved asymmetrically are very important, or go to a very large constituent unit, this can create pressure to limit the weight of representatives from that unit in the central government's decision making on these subjects. In practice, most constitutional asymmetries of powers in federations are of relatively secondary powers or special arrangements for very small and recognizably distinct constituent units. (This is different from the lesser legal status of territories or tribal areas and of national capitals in some federations.) A number of federations do have non-constitutional arrangements that permit some asymmetry in the administrative or policy responsibilities of constituent units.

Examples of Asymmetrical Distribution of Powers in Federations

Virtually all the long-established federations allocate the same legislative powers to their individual constituent units. However, in **Canada**, the federal parliament's powers over property and civil rights vary by province; moreover, Quebec effectively has non-constitutional arrangements with the federal government, which give it different authority from—though usually harmonized with—that given to the other provinces (e.g., pensions, taxes, social programs). Of the newer federations, **Malaysia** provides the Borneo states special powers over native laws, communications, fisheries, forestry, and immigration. **India** has similar provisions for Jammu and Kashmir and some of the smaller states. **Russia** made extensive use of very different non-constitutional bilateral agreements with constituent units of the federation that tended to favour certain powerful units, but these variations have now been largely eliminated. **Spain** also engaged in bilateral arrangements, notably in giving special powers to the autonomous communities that had historic nationalities; again, the differences have greatly diminished over time, with the exception of ancient historic fiscal rights for the Basque country and Navarre. **Belgium, Comoros, Bosnia and Herzegovina**, and **St. Kitts and Nevis** also have some constitutionalized asymmetrical arrangements. Perhaps the most significant such asymmetrical arrangements are with Scotland in the **United Kingdom**, which is not a federation; the implications of this are still being debated in the UK. The **European Union** has member states that are not part of the monetary union.

Dealing with conflicts over powers

Federations can deal with conflicts over the distribution of powers by using the courts, emergency powers, constitutional amendments, political compromise, and elections.

The classic way to resolve differences over how to interpret the division of powers is by reference to the courts, though a few federations have more political processes such as referendums and upper houses. Many federations also have special provisions—the most extreme being emergency powers—that permit the federal government in certain circumstances, notably emergencies, to suspend the normal authority of the government in a constituent unit.

Very often, the conflict is not over the legal interpretation of what the powers are, but over what the respective powers or roles of the two orders should be. Such disputes must be addressed politically. The governments can negotiate to try to reach an agreement on how to operate within the existing constitution. Or they may agree to amend the constitution, which in most federations requires a special majority (and not always the consent of the constituent unit governments). Where governments cannot agree, they (or the different political parties) can take their respective cases to the population during elections to seek support for their views.

Chapter Five

Money and Fiscal Powers

The importance of money

Arrangements around the raising, sharing, and spending of money are critically important, both politically and economically, for the functioning of federal systems.

The truism that money matters applies as much in federal systems as it does in life generally.

First, arrangements around who determines and collects taxes and other revenues and who spends them, how, and on what are fundamental to the real division of powers in a federal system. They can significantly alter the apparent legislative powers of the two orders of government. In particular, central governments often use their very strong fiscal powers to influence or control constituent-unit governments in various ways.

Second, the ways in which money is raised and spent can significantly affect the economic health of a federation.

- **Tax and spending incentives** affect the efficiency and performance of the economy. They can be used by constituent units to try to attract businesses and citizens to locate and invest within their boundaries. While some tax and spending competition can be healthy, it can also be costly in attracting economic activity to inefficient locations and causing a loss or misuse of revenues.

- **Revenue raising** (taxes, charges, debt, issuance of money) **and**

spending by governments affects the total level of activity in the economy whether policies are expansionary or contractionary. Some federations have had major problems managing coherent fiscal and monetary policies, with serious bouts of inflation and exaggerated economic cycles of boom or bust.

Fiscal and monetary powers are important both economically and in their larger impact on the roles of the two orders of government.

Assignment of revenue powers

There are principles for the effective assignment of revenue-raising powers between governments in federations. In practice, however, there is great variation, largely because the constitutional arrangements, histories of revenue raising, and political cultures of countries can be so different.

Many economists argue that a federation should minimize the extent to which constituent units use tax competition to influence companies and individuals to locate in a particular area. This suggests constituent units (and local governments) should have limited control over mobile taxpayers and tax bases (such as corporate and personal income tax and sales taxes). Instead, they should be given power over property taxes because property does not move. In practice, the mobility of taxpayers or taxable activity depends on cultural factors (are citizens very attached to living in their constituent unit?), on distance (is it easy to work or shop in another jurisdiction?), on geographic endowment (natural resources) and on technology (new technologies offer new locational choices).

At the same time, some economists favour fairly extensive tax competition (along with other kinds of competition in public policies) because they believe it can promote better policies: it is a potential advantage of federalism. Some economists argue that constituent units should have the right to vary the rates of personal and corporate taxes, but that it is economically efficient to have one (federally or jointly decided) structure for these taxes. There is no one answer about the best allocation of tax powers within federations. Too much competition between jurisdictions over taxes on mobile factors can lead to a downward spiral of tax rates, with a loss of revenues from some tax bases and a need to focus taxes more on other tax bases. But some competition can be positive.

There are other considerations about how best to assign tax and revenue powers:

- There are advantages to making governments accountable for the money they spend, and it is usually argued that they will be more accountable to their electors if they have to raise most of their revenues themselves.

- There are also equity considerations related to whether poorer constituent units should be expected to have a greater tax effort, lower services, or transfers to assist them.

- There can be administrative advantages to centralizing certain kinds of revenue collection, even if the revenue base belongs to constituent units.

Some federations are rich in natural resources, which can provide large revenues or rents, especially from oil, gas, diamonds, and some metals. Such resources are typically very unevenly distributed between constituent units, causing tension within the federation. In some cases, the central government owns these resources; in others, it is the constituent-unit governments (or, rarely, private landowners): in either case, there can be debates about who collects what revenues from natural resources, how resource revenues should be distributed, and how much the distribution of resource revenues should affect the distribution of other revenues.

Natural Resource Revenues in Some Federations

Natural-resource revenues come principally from royalties, licence fees, export taxes, and corporate taxes. They are by far the largest source of revenues in **Nigeria**, where the central government collects them, and then makes transfers to the states based on principles of equity and derivation (more for the producing states). In **Russia**, both royalties and export taxes are important, and the central government now dominates their collection with some small advantage for producing constituent units. **Argentina** transferred resources to the provinces and some small, resource-rich provinces now enjoy a substantial fiscal advantage. In **Canada**, Alberta (like other provinces) owns its resources and has almost twice the revenue-raising capacity of other provinces; the federal government has lost its power to apply export taxes to energy exports. In the **United States**, most resources are owned by the states or private individuals, but there are extensive federal lands in the Western states and Alaska. **Sudan** has a petroleum revenue-sharing arrangement that gives the larger share to South Sudan, which has a smaller population but is the main source of production. In most federations, the federal government owns and controls offshore resources and their revenues; in **Canada** the offshore provinces have been given the benefits of offshore revenues.

While various principles and considerations can help shape the revenue-raising system in a federation, the actual systems have been strongly influenced by several factors: the constitutional allocation of revenue powers, the history of which government has occupied which tax field, and the political culture of the country, which can favour competitiveness or conformity, as well as more, or less, centralization. The resulting revenue arrangements vary considerably across federations; in some, the central government dominates the levying and collection of revenues, while in others, the central, constituent-unit and local governments all play a significant role.

Central-government revenues relative to total-government revenues across federations

In **Canada** and **Switzerland**, the central government collects around 45 per cent of total revenues, and in the United States, 54 per cent. There is a cluster of federations (**Austria, Australia, Belgium, Brazil, India, Germany**, and **Spain**) in which the central government collects between 60 to 75 per cent of total revenues. And there are some federations (**Argentina, Malaysia, Mexico, Nigeria, Russia, South Africa**, and **Venezuela**) where the federal government levies and collects over 80 per cent of revenues. Nigeria and **Venezuela** are the most extreme cases, with central revenues of 98 and 97 per cent respectively. **The European Union** is not a federation and its central revenues are less than two per cent of total government revenues. Some non-federations are more decentralized in regards to raising revenue than are some highly centralized federations.

Fiscal balance between orders of government

Federations vary greatly in the extent of direct government spending done by the central, constituent-unit and local governments respectively.

In some federations, the federal government dominates the delivery of programs, while, in others, constituent-unit and local-government expenditures are larger. These differences reflect constitutional arrangements, priorities in government spending (e.g., defence versus social programs), and political history and culture.

Central-Government Direct Spending Relative to Total-Government Spending Across Federations

Switzerland, Canada, Belgium, and **Germany** are the federations where central government spending is smallest (30 to 40 per cent) as a share of total government spending. In the German case, this is because the *Länder* are responsible for delivering many federally legislated programs, while in the case of **Switzerland, Canada**, and **Belgium**, it reflects the importance of the responsibilities of the constituent units. Central direct spending in most federations (**Argentina, Australia, Austria, India, Mexico, Nigeria, Russia, Spain, South Africa, and the United States**) falls between 45 to 60 per cent, and Brazil, at 64 per cent, is just above this. At the extreme are **Malaysia** (84 per cent) and **Venezuela** (78 per cent). **Mexico, Nigeria, and Spain** were very centralized but have devolved spending significantly in recent years.

Central transfers to constituent units

In all federations, the central government raises more revenue than it spends for its own needs. This enables it to make fiscal transfers to the constituent-unit governments.

Federations vary in the degree to which revenue collection and program spending are centralized. But in all federations, the central government raises more revenues (including through borrowing) than it needs for its own direct spending, partly because of the advantages of significantly centralized revenue collection. Central governments make fiscal transfers to the constituent units—and sometimes directly to local governments—to enable them to better meet their responsibilities. The importance of these transfers varies: while in some federations constituent units depend overwhelmingly on transfers, in most federations, central transfers to the constituent units cover, on average, less than half of their spending. As a consequence, most federations have a fair measure of accountability by constituent governments to their populations for the revenues they raise relative to programs.

There can be heated debates in federations about whether the allocation of revenue raising, transfers, and responsibilities is fair. There is no simple technical solution to this because it depends in large measure on political judgments about priorities for public spending. The vertical fiscal gap is a term used for the difference between the spending of constituent units and their own source revenues.

Central Transfers Relative to Constituent-Unit Spending

The smallest central transfers relative to total constituent-unit spending are in **Canada, Switzerland,** and the **United States** (around 13 to 26 per cent); Russia and Malaysia have relatively low transfers (23 and 30 per cent respectively) in a context of highly centralized program spending, reflecting the weakness of their constituent units. Germany has significant revenue sharing, which brings total transfers there to 44 per cent. The **Australian** and **Indian** central governments are large funders of constituent units (46 per cent in both). **Spain** (73 per cent) and **Belgium** (68 per cent) provide large transfers since they are recent federations that have devolved program responsibilities far more than revenue powers. At the extreme are **South Africa**, **Nigeria**, and **Mexico**, where the constituent units are dependent on central transfers for more than 87 per cent of their revenues.

Fiscal inequality and equalization

The wealth of constituent units within federations differs greatly, affecting their ability to raise own-source revenues. Most federations have provisions for dealing with these differences through greater transfers to poorer constituent units. There is great variation in the design and underlying principles for such transfer arrangements.

All countries have regional differences in wealth. Federations face a particular challenge in that the governments of the constituent units typically have the same or almost the same responsibilities, but they can have very different abilities to raise required revenues. Consequently, these governments would be able to provide programs of very unequal quality and scale if limited to their own revenues.

Federations deal with this problem in varied ways. Most federations (the US is a notable exception) use the principle of equalization, namely that there should be mechanisms to even up the revenues available to the different constituent-unit governments. Set against this, there is also a principle of derivation, namely that the jurisdiction that is the source of a particular revenue may have a special claim to all or part of that revenue: this principle is often invoked in relation to resource revenues (whatever the constitutional arrangements). Clearly there is a conflict between the equalization and derivation principles, and federations give quite different weight to each principle.

Most federations have some kind of equalization program that provides transfers from the central government to the constituent-unit governments (though in Germany and Switzerland it also includes transfers directly from the governments of richer constituent units to their poorer counterparts). These programs vary in their underlying approach.

- Some programs shrink gaps only in revenue capacity, which measures the ability to raise revenues, while others try to address revenue effort and revenue needs as well.

- Some rich federations bring all units to the same level (100 per cent equalization), while others bring them only within a broad range. (Germany did even more, with massive transfers—effectively super-equalization—to permit the Eastern *Länder* to rebuild after reunification.)

- Some equalize only the poorer constituent units up to a standard, while others equalize all units, up and down, to a standard.

Equalization programs provide unconditional transfers, which the receiving governments can use for any purpose. In most federations, conditional transfers also play an important role; the central government attaches conditions to the purposes and manner in which these transfers are used. Conditional transfers are program specific so they may not contribute to equalizing the positions of constituent governments.

In many federations, there is debate over the size of unconditional versus conditional transfers: unconditional transfers tend to favour the independence of constituent-unit governments, while conditional transfers promote the achievement of national purposes and standards, e.g., health. The United States is the great outlier in having no equalization program: all federal transfers are conditional; some have equalizing features, but the sum of federal transfers has no systematic equalizing impact.

Central governments also spend significant amounts on their own direct programs, so the regional location of central government spending can affect fiscal redistribution. No federation has explicit rules on this and it can be difficult to get good statistics on where exactly money is spent or who benefits from a particular expenditure (e.g., a military base in a constituent unit is protecting the whole country; a piece of machinery bought in one region for use in another benefits both). However, the regional impact of central government spending, especially large strategic investments, is frequently a political issue in federal systems. Social payments by central governments, such as on pensions and unemployment insurance, can have a large impact on interregional transfers and levels of inequality.

Finally, views differ on the economic implications of equalization programs:

- Advocates argue that they ensure comparable infrastructure and services throughout the federation, which is important for regional development as well as a high-quality workforce. They can also compensate for the lack of labour mobility caused by regional language differences.

- Critics argue that they drain money from the most competitive parts of a country and slow deeper structural adjustments, such as population movements from poorer regions.

Most federations seem sensitive to both arguments and fall somewhere between 'very ambitious' and 'no equalization'. Richer federations can usually afford a higher standard of equalization because the differences in wealth between their constituent units are much less than in transitional and developing-country federations. The design of equalization programs can affect the incentives for constituent governments to raise their own taxes and promote economic growth.

The Spending Power

Federations differ in the approach to spending by central governments in areas beyond their legislative jurisdiction. The spending power of a government can have important implications for the character of a federation.

All federations have a legislative division of powers that constrains, at least to some extent, each order of government from making laws in areas of the others' jurisdiction. However, they normally allow spending in the area of another government's exclusive legislative jurisdiction. Central governments frequently use this spending power to influence the programs and activities of constituent units, notably through conditional grants and shared-cost programs.

> ### Legal Provisions around Spending Power in Some Federations
>
> The constitutions of **Australia, India,** and **Malaysia** explicitly grant the central government the right to spend in areas beyond their jurisdiction (as does that of **Spain,** though subject to restrictive court interpretations). The **United States** Constitution gives the central government a power to levy taxes for general welfare, which has been interpreted broadly as no legal limit on federal spending. In **Canada,** court interpretation has given both orders of government unlimited spending powers, but there is a federal-provincial agreement that new federal-spending initiatives in areas of provincial competence would require majority support from the provinces and allow opting out by individual provinces, subject to certain conditions. The **Swiss** Constitution generally does not permit central spending in areas of exclusive cantonal jurisdiction, but, in practice, the only check on such spending would be through the use of referendums, not court rulings, and this has not happened. **Germany** is characterized by large areas of concurrent or joint jurisdiction, and many federal laws are administered by the *Länder*. all decisions on such spending require a majority of *Länder* in the Bundesrat, where the votes of individual *Länder* are weighted. **Belgium** is rare in that it explicitly limits spending to areas of legislative competence.

While the use of the spending power for unconditional transfers is usually relatively uncontroversial, constituent units frequently object to its use for conditional transfers. There are several reasons:

- Central government conditions can effectively dictate the programs of constituent units in areas of their exclusive competency.

- Central government grants can distort constituent-unit priorities by requiring matching funds as a condition of receiving the grants.

- A central government can withdraw or reduce such transfers once a program is established by the constituent units, leaving them to deal with public expectations.

- Discretionary grants to constituent units can be used by the central government to favour its political friends and punish its adversaries, and even to distort electoral outcomes.

Against this, defenders of the spending power argue that it is different in kind from the legislative power. There is not the same need to establish paramountcy for spending because both orders of government can spend in the same area without creating a clear conflict or impasse. However, the main defence is that the spending power enables a federation to adapt and respond to changing circumstances and national needs.

Both sets of arguments have some validity, but, in practice, the spending power is a major feature of the operation of virtually all federations. So often the issue is over *how* it is used, not *whether*.

- There can be **formal** (Germany) or **informal** (Canada) rules requiring some level of constituent-unit consent. Canada has even experimented with opting-out arrangements for provinces that do not agree with an initiative.

- There can be **varied degrees of conditionality** so as to give constituent units more flexibility to design programs that conform to a broad national standard or purpose. Once programs are established, this can even extend to converting conditional grants into unconditional block transfers.

Conditionality and Spending Powers in Some Federations

In the **United States**, all transfers to states are conditional and they account for about 30 per cent of state-level revenues. In Mexico, 49 per cent of state revenues and, in **Spain**, 42 per cent of autonomous communities' revenues are conditional transfers. By contrast, **Canada**, **Belgium**, and **Russia** are at the other extreme with four or less per cent of their transfers being conditional (though, in Canada, many important social programs were originally started on a conditional basis and some current transfers are subject to very broad principles and reporting requirements). Conditional transfers are important in **Australia**, **India**, and **Switzerland**, where they account for 17 to 20 per cent of total revenues of constituent units. They are used as well to a lesser extent in **Germany** and **Malaysia**.

Chapter Six

Political Institutions of the Central Government

Importance and variety of central institutions

The political institutions—legislative, executive, administrative, and partisan—at the centre of a federation help define and shape the character of the federation. The institutional arrangements within the constituent units and the central government are usually of the same type.

Central governments in federations are made up of formal and informal institutions and practices, which, in turn, strongly affect the nature and functioning not just of the central government but of the whole federation.

Such institutions can:

- be parliamentary or presidential in form;

- give considerable weight to regional or special group representation;

- use majoritarian or proportional electoral systems;

- feature one dominant political party, two alternating parties, or multiple parties of very different sizes; and,

- have a partisan, political culture of winner-takes-all, or one of consensus with broadly based governments and decision making.

In order to maintain their legitimacy and effectiveness, central governments should meet their constitutional responsibilities, foster national unity, develop national identity, protect rights and minorities, and promote the healthy functioning of the federation. In practice, their success, or even their commitment to these goals, can depend heavily on the choice of institutional arrangements and practices.

Federations typically adopt the same type of legislative and executive institutions (parliamentary or presidential) for both orders of government (though upper houses are the exception in constituent units). By contrast, the electoral regimes and party systems can differ at the two levels, though the norm is for similar electoral rules and political parties that operate at both levels.

Parliamentary, presidential, and mixed regimes

Both parliamentary and presidential-congressional regimes, as well as mixed variants, demonstrate great variety in terms of their actual functioning. In practice, either can result in a concentration of power within the executive branches or a dispersal of power in which both the executives and the legislatures play significant independent roles. In the former case, intergovernmental relations are characterized by executive federalism.

Federations can have parliamentary, presidential-congressional, or mixed institutions in both orders of government. In parliamentary regimes, the cabinet (executive) is largely drawn from the legislature and must keep the confidence of the lower house to stay in office. In presidential regimes, the president is elected by the population, and the president names the cabinet (perhaps with some measure of legislative ratification). Neither the president nor the cabinet requires the confidence of the legislature to remain in office. There are important variations on these models in Russia, South Africa, and Switzerland.

The presidential-congressional model is based on a separation of powers between the executive and the legislature, while the parliamentary model integrates the two. Parliamentary systems produce very strong executives when one party controls a majority in the legislature and the cabinet can be assured that its legislative proposals are adopted. Even when there are coalition governments, party leaders in cabinet can have substantial control over their members in parliament. Presidential systems can have much weaker executives because the president's party may not control the congress—and even if it does, party members may be much more independent than they typically are in parliamentary regimes.

In practice, either system can produce executives that are strong and largely in control of the legislature, or weak and heavily dependent upon it. The actual situation will depend on constitutional rules (e.g., powers of the executive vs. those of the legislature) as well as the state of the party system. Some constitutions give the executive (notably a president) exceptional powers, e.g., to issue decrees, relative to the legislature. In competitive politics, the party system is central. If the governing party is dominant, it can control both branches of government, while if it is weak, it can require the cooperation of other parties: thus executives can be strong or weak in either presidential or parliamentary regimes.

Design of Legislative and Executive Institutions in Some Federations

The **United States**, **Argentina**, **Brazil**, **Mexico**, **Venezuela**, and **Nigeria** all have presidential regimes (Nigeria previously had a parliamentary regime), but they differ substantially. Argentina and Venezuela have exceptionally strong presidents compared to the others. **Australia**, **Austria**, **Belgium**, **Canada**, **Germany**, **India**, **Malaysia**, and **Spain** have parliamentary institutions. **South Africa** has a mixed regime, under which the president is elected by the parliament as both head of state and of government, and does not sit in parliament. **Russia** also has a mixed regime, in which the president is elected by the population, but the government needs the confidence of the parliament.

Switzerland has a seven-member executive elected by the parliament, which then serves independently of parliamentary confidence for its term; the executive represents all major parties.

In federations with strong executives, the executive branch tends to dominate relations between the central government and the constituent-unit governments—leading to what is known as executive federalism.

Strongly Concentrated Power within the Central Governments of Some Federations

Argentina and **Venezuela** are sometimes called hyper-presidential because the president controls so many levers. In Argentina, the president has extensive authority to issue legislative decrees and to direct fiscal transfers to the provinces. In federations with strong one-party dominance of both the central and constituent-unit governments (**South Africa, Ethiopia, India** for a period after independence, **Mexico** under the Institutional Revolutionary Party or PRI), key decisions tend to be made within the governing party, whether the system is parliamentary, presidential, or mixed, and the formal institutions largely execute the party leaders' decisions. **Russia** increasingly has one dominant party at both levels and an exceptionally powerful president. **Malaysia** has strong one-party dominance at the centre, with an opposition party controlling only one state.

Upper houses and territorial representation

The central legislatures of federations usually have some balancing of representation by population with representation by constituent units. This federal dimension of representation is usually embodied in upper houses, but it can be present in lower houses as well. The method for selecting members of the upper house and the powers of the upper house differs greatly among federations, with important consequences for the functioning of federations.

Many countries, federal and non-federal, have two houses in their legislatures. In federations, these two houses

- are always constituted on different representative principles, with the upper house usually using a formula based on constituent units and the lower house allocating membership closer to representation by population;

- are elected or named in different ways; and,

- can have quite similar or very distinct powers.

There is no consistent pattern across federations on these matters. However, in parliamentary regimes, the lower house is usually the confidence chamber that determines who forms the government.

Principles of representation

Almost all federations have an upper house whose membership is in some way representative of the constituent units. The prevalence of such upper houses in federations is associated with the idea that both the population and the constituent units are part of what makes a federation, and both dimensions need to be reflected in the central institutions.

Representation in the upper house is frequently based on equal representation for each constituent unit, but many federations have allocations that take into account differences in population (e.g., big units getting two or three times the number of representatives of small units). A few federations elect some upper-house members as representatives of constituent units and other as representatives of one or more alternative constituencies (a national list; a non-geographic community).

Where they are elected directly, members of upper houses usually have longer terms than members of the lower house, and their electoral district is often the whole constituent unit, while lower-house members come from smaller districts. This gives a different political character to elected members in the two houses. In some federations, members of the upper house are indirectly elected by the legislature of the constituent unit (or, in a few, by a combination of direct and indirect election). Directly, and even indirectly, elected upper houses usually play a relatively small role in representing the interests and views of the governments of the constituent units.

The upper house that plays the most distinctive federal role is probably the Bundesrat in Germany, which is not elected: *Länder* delega-

tions are named by their governments and officially led by their min-
ister-presidents. Legislation that affects the *Länder* (now about 40 per
cent of all legislation) must be approved by the Bundesrat, which
means that the central government needs a weighted majority of these
governments to pass such acts. The Bundesrat is thus central to intergovernmental relations. The unique, interlocking nature of German
federalism has given both orders of government a huge stake in who
controls other governments, with consequent interlocking of federal
and land parties.

Finally, in many federations, there are also provisions that give extra
weight to representation from smaller constituent units in the lower
house. These can guarantee a minimum (or even a maximum) number of representatives in the lower house. Typically, such extra weight-
ing for smaller units occurs much less in lower houses than in upper
houses, but it can be significant, with Brazil being the most dramatic
example. Whether in upper or lower houses, elected members typically vote more along party than regional lines: the advantage to smaller
units of their extra representation in legislatures is that it can help tip
the balance of votes towards parties they favour.

Representation in Lower and Upper Houses in Some Federations

**Argentina, Australia, Brazil, Nigeria, Mexico, Russia, South
Africa, Switzerland,** and the **United States,** all have an equal
number of members in their upper house from each full constituent unit. **Austria, Belgium, Canada, Ethiopia, Germany,**
and **India** have unequal representation by constituent units,
with weight given to population differences. **Spain** represents
all mainland provinces equally, but varies representation of
autonomous communities (states) by population. **Mexico** gives
all states equal representation, but elects one-quarter of senators
nationally by proportional representation.

Most federations elect members of their upper house directly,
but a number (Austria, Belgium, India, Spain) elect all or some
indirectly. The Russian and South African upper houses have
representatives named by both the executives and the legisla-

tures in the constituent units. Germany's *Länder* governments appoint delegations to the Bundesrat. In **Malaysia**, state legislatures name 38 per cent of members of the upper house, while minorities name the others. Canada has never succeeded in significantly reforming its unelected Senate to which the federal government names unelected senators to serve until 75 years of age. In Switzerland and Ethiopia, constituent-unit legislatures decide how to select their members of the national upper house. **Venezuela** has no upper house.

The effective weight of representatives from small constituent units varies a good deal by federation. **Brazil** represents one extreme, where senators from states having eight per cent of the population hold over 50 per cent of the seats. In **Russia**, the smallest unit is 1/450th the size of the largest unit, with both having equal representation in the upper house. Some federations also have special provisions for the number of representatives from constituent units in their lower house. **Brazil** is again notable in the extent to which it caps the number of representatives from the largest state of Sao Paulo, and guarantees a minimum number from the smallest states.

Powers of upper houses

There is no consistent pattern in the powers assigned to upper houses in federations. In some federations, they have both all the powers of the lower house and special additional powers; for example, over treaties, declarations of war, and high appointments. At the other extreme, some upper houses are little more than revisionary chambers, with limited powers to amend or delay some legislation (and possibly subject to an override by the lower house).

The range of arrangements includes those affecting the scope of an upper house's powers (types of legislation and government action it can affect) and the strength of these powers (veto, delay, right to force a joint sitting of both houses to resolve a deadlock—which favours the more numerous lower house). Some upper houses are designed to play a role in federal matters, such as legislation affecting the constituent units or specified minorities or rights. While almost all federations have some kind of upper house (Venezuela does not), many of these have quite minor powers or weak legitimacy because of how they are selected.

Powers of Upper Houses in Some Federations

The **United States** Senate has all the powers of the House of Representatives, but it alone can approve key appointments, declarations of war, and treaties. The **Argentine, Australian, Brazilian** and **Swiss** upper houses have an absolute veto over all legislation (though, in Australia, a deadlock can be broken by a joint sitting of both houses after a special election). The **German** Bundesrat has a veto over matters affecting *Länder* (now about 40 per cent of laws), and a suspensive veto on other matters. The **Indian and Nigerian** upper houses have a veto that can be overridden by a majority in a joint sitting of the two houses. The **Austrian, Malaysian, and Spanish** upper houses have suspensive vetoes only. The **Canadian** Senate has extensive legal powers, but, because it lacks political legitimacy, it uses its powers mainly to revise and delay. The **Ethiopian** House of the Federation plays no role in normal legislation, but can reject a budget on the grounds of its fiscal allocations to states; it also addresses disputes between states and acts as a final interpreter of the constitution.

Political parties

Political parties are basic to the functioning of federations. The character of parties and of the party system reflects political cleavages within the population and partisan history, but is also significantly shaped by electoral laws and constitutional arrangements. Federations vary in having one dominant party, two or more major, or many parties. Usually parties operating at the federal level are linked to parties within the constituent units, but there are exceptions.

Political parties and electoral laws in federal systems, while not usually part of the constitution, play a critical role in determining how a written constitution operates in practice. As well, political parties can change much more quickly than a written constitution. The functioning and character of some federations have changed quite dramatically as the political party system has evolved, even though the constitution may be unchanged. This has been particularly true in countries that shift from a dominant party—such as Congress in India or the PRI in Mexico—to a more pluralistic and competitive system of parties.

The two main variants of electoral regimes are proportional representation on the one hand and majoritarian or plurality regimes on the other. There are also mixed regimes.

- **Proportional representation** (PR) regimes tend to be based on relatively large, multi-member electoral districts in which voters choose between party lists, but there are many variations. A key issue in such regimes is the minimum threshold or share of the vote that is needed to elect a representative. In some cases, this is a defined share of the national vote (e.g., five per cent). In other cases, it is simply a result of the number of representatives being elected from a district: the more representatives, the smaller the proportion of the vote necessary to get elected.

- **Majoritarian or plurality regimes** tend to be based on one-member electoral districts where the candidate with the largest vote (a plurality) is the winner. In some cases, the top two candidates meet in a second round of voting to determine the winner.

- **Mixed regimes** elect some members in a majoritarian way from single-member constituencies, and others on the basis of votes cast for the parties. The effect on overall representation in the legislature is usually dominated by the rules of proportionality.

Historically, federations with common-law and British constitutional antecedents have tended to have majoritarian electoral laws, while continental and civil-law federations have opted for PR regimes, but there are numerous exceptions. As well, direct elections of presidents must be done by some variation of a majoritarian regime, even if PR is used in the legislature. Some federations use different electoral rules for the lower and upper houses, when both are directly elected.

It is usually said that PR regimes lead to more splintered party systems than do majoritarian regimes, but this depends a great deal on precise rules (such as the height of the minimum threshold) and on the characteristics of the voter base supporting different parties. Thus some federations with PR have only two or three significant parties. However, it is rare in a PR regime for one party to win enough votes to have a majority in the legislature, so parliamentary federations with PR typically have multi-party coalition governments.

Majoritarian regimes frequently make it possible for a party with substantially less than a majority of the vote to win a majority of seats. Thus parliamentary federations with majoritarian electoral laws more often have one-party government (though the party in power may change with some regularity). While majoritarian electoral systems generally give parties with larger vote shares a disproportionately large number of seats, much depends on the regional distribution of votes. Smaller parties that are regionally concentrated can also benefit from majoritarian systems. In such federations as India and Canada, regionally based parties sometimes have a much larger share of seats than of votes, thus raising the importance of regional (or local ethnic, religious, or language) demands on the national stage.

A critical issue in a federation is the electoral base of the various political parties. Such parties can have strong or weak links to class, religion, ethnicity, or region; they can be narrowly or broadly based. Typically, the challenge of managing a federation is greater if regionally based parties are very strong.

Party Systems in Some Federations

While two parties have dominated **United States** politics for over a century (no third party has lasted), their electoral bases and character have shifted considerably, particularly in the South, which started to defect from the Democrats following the Civil Rights Act in the 1960s. The **Australian** party system, also dominated by two parties, has been remarkably stable. The **Canadian** party system has shown much more volatility, with major swings in support for the two major parties and with regional or nationalist parties having extended periods of importance. The **German** system has been relatively stable with two large parties, but increasingly smaller parties are a factor because of new issues (environment) and unification with East Germany.

India and Mexico were long dominated by one party at both levels of government. India now has a highly fractured system requiring large, multi-party coalitions to form a government, while Mexico's recent presidents have had to work with a congress controlled by the opposition. In **South Africa**, the African National Congress continues to dominate both orders of government. **Nigeria's** recent history of electoral politics has seen one large party and a fractured but significant opposition. **Spain** has a competitive system of two major parties, but both must rely on smaller, regionally based parties if they are to form a government. **Belgium's** old party system, based on left-right divisions, has fractured further along communal lines, but coalitions tend to cross the communal divisions. **Switzerland's** system, based on broad coalitions and consensus, is being tested by the rise of the Swiss People's Party. **Argentina's** democracy has been disrupted by periods of military rule, but the party system is volatile, reflecting the presidential character of its politics. In **Russia**, a dominant presidential party has emerged from a formerly fractured party system.

Provisions regarding minorities

Whatever their party systems, federations differ in their approaches to accommodation of regional and ethnic minorities within central decision-making institutions. Inclusion can reflect the power of minorities in coalition building, it can be a matter of political culture or established practice, or it can be prescribed in the constitution. Giving minorities a real voice in central institutions can be important in promoting social harmony and political stability.

We have seen that the composition of constituent units in a federation can be important for empowering and accommodating territorially concentrated populations with a strong, distinct identity. However, even if such a population is a regional majority in one constituent unit, it may still not identify with the whole federation if it has the sense of not being properly treated and included in the central political and administrative institutions of the federation.

Federations vary in the extent to which such minorities find effective political voice within central institutions, whether via political parties or other means. Some federations have a relatively consensual approach to politics, while others have a more majoritarian approach (sometimes called 'winner-take-all'). Differences between countries in this regard reflect their political culture, but also their institutions.

A key question is whether presidential or parliamentary systems are better designed to facilitate and accommodate the inclusion of minorities within the central government:

- Presidential systems involve one winner as head of government, but they can have practices or rules to ensure that the cabinet and other high offices are broadly representative of the country. And the power of a president can be constrained if the legislature is independent—especially if opposition parties are important within it—and endowed with real powers of its own. Most ethnically diverse federations do not have presidential regimes (Nigeria being a notable exception).

- Parliamentary systems can be majoritarian, especially with plurality regimes and single-member constituencies where one party can win a majority on its own. However, even then, large governing parties often have a broad representation so that a minority may be part of their electoral base. Parliamentary systems can also have many smaller parties, sometimes based in ethnic, religious, or linguistic communities, and then the issue is how a government coalition is put together.

Minority Accommodation in the Central Governments of Some Federations with Ethnic, Linguistic, or Religious Diversity

Canada has a majoritarian parliamentary regime, but the French-Canadian minority has normally played an important role in any Cabinet. **India's** government is increasingly formed of large coalitions including many small parties that represent different communities. **Switzerland** has a very consensual approach where all majority parties jointly form the government. **Belgium's** governments are required by the constitution to be coalitions that cross linguistic lines. **Spain's** parliamentary governments tend to require the support of at least one regionally based party along with one of the two large national parties. **Nigeria's** presidential regime requires that the President and Vice-President always come from different regions (and in practice religions) and that the Cabinet must include a member from every state.

Beyond the central political institutions, policies can promote (or discourage) minority participation or representation in the army, the civil service, and the courts. Minority languages can be given official status so that minority citizens can be served by the central government or courts in their language and, in some cases, so that they can work in these institutions in their language.

Chapter Seven

The Legal Pillars of Federalism

The constitutional basis of federalism

Effective federal governance must be based on a written constitution and the rule of law. The constitution sets the basic framework and principles of the federation. A constitution can be symbolically important in fostering unity or discord within the country. Constitutions vary greatly in their length, specificity, and accessibility.

Written constitutions are essential in federations to establish the framework within which each order of government operates. At a minimum, the constitution must establish certain key institutions and allocations of responsibility within the federal system.

Federal constitutions vary enormously. The older federations usually have much shorter constitutions than those created since the middle of the twentieth century. These older constitutions were written before modern government and often are silent or elliptical on current major responsibilities of government, such as environmental management. Moreover, their allocation of powers can rely heavily on a few basic principles (e.g., residual powers, national interest, trade and commerce) whose interpretation may have evolved very differently from the original intentions of the constitution's authors. Shorter constitutions tend to be more flexible than those with very detailed lists of powers for the different orders of government.

There is a large measure of choice as to what is put into a constitution or left to ordinary laws. This can lead to major debates because advocates can seek to constitutionalize provisions to give them symbolic recognition, or the extra protection of constitutional protection, or both. Constitutional provisions around the definition of the country, the recognition of minority nationalities, language rights, and religion can be very important in dividing or uniting a population around the constitution. In more recent constitutions, there are often long sections on social and economic rights. Ideally, there should be broad consensus around constitutional provisions because it is the 'basic law': this is the reason for special thresholds for constitutional amendment.

Constitutional arbitration

Two independent orders of government in a federation create a need for a constitutional arbiter to resolve conflicts over their respective constitutional competencies. This role is usually assigned to the courts.

A federal constitution must provide a method for resolving possible conflicts over the legal powers of the two orders of government. A citizen or company can obey only one of two contradictory laws. Legal conflicts can arise in different ways:

- When both orders of government have concurrent legal authority over a subject, the laws of one order must prevail in cases of conflict; thus constitutions indicate which order has paramountcy. Normally the central government's laws are paramount, but there are exceptions (e.g., provincial laws on pensions prevail in Canada).

- Both orders may pass laws that conflict, and defend their respective laws as deriving from distinct powers. For example, the central government might have a power over internal trade, while the constituent-unit governments have the power over property, and they pass conflicting laws relating to these two areas. In such a case, resolving the conflict requires determining which power—internal trade or property—is the more relevant.

- Sometimes there is no actual conflict between two laws, but a government or private interest objects to a law passed by another government on the grounds that the law exceeds its legal jurisdiction.

- Sometimes, the objection is on the grounds that the law contravenes a constitutionally established right.

A strong, autonomous judiciary is crucial for the rule of law. Within most federations, the judiciary, in particular the highest or constitutional court, has the ultimate authority for resolving constitutional disputes. Resolving such disputes can put a high court in the sometimes difficult position of rejecting an action or law that a powerful government considers important.

At least two federations do not give all aspects of final arbitration on the constitution to their high court. The Swiss federation, which is based on the concept that ultimate sovereignty rests with the people, decides on the validity of contested federal (not cantonal) laws by referendum. In Ethiopia, the House of the Federation, elected by the state legislatures, has final authority, subject to legal advice from judges.

Emergency and special non-federal powers

In some federations, the central government or its executive can override normal constitutional arrangements in special circumstances, such as emergencies. While justified in limited circumstances, such powers can be abused to circumvent the spirit of constitutional government. The political evolution of some federations has constrained the use of such powers or rendered them obsolete.

Some federations have been deemed quasi-federal because their central governments have extraordinary powers to intervene in the jurisdiction of constituent units. These can take the form of an emergency power, in which the central government may suspend the government in a constituent unit. They can be a general directive power, or a power of suspension, or of disallowance. In each case, there is a question of what constitutional techniques might constrain the central government's use of such powers: the courts might have a role in judging the emergency, or the use of the power may require the consent of legislators—though this can have limited effectiveness if the head of government's allies control the legislature; South Africa's constitution is probably the most developed in specifying protections. Over time, originally quasi-federal countries, such as Canada and India, have evolved away from the use of such powers. However, they have been used extensively to weaken some federations, such as Argentina.

Emergency and Override Powers in Some Federations

Constitutionally, the **Canadian** central government can disallow provincial legislation before it is enacted and declare any work or undertaking to be federal, but in practice these powers are obsolete. In **India**, a state government can be removed and replaced by President's rule. While this power was intended for emergencies or a breakdown of constitutional government, it was used for partisan purposes and is now subject to greater discipline by the courts and India's political culture. Under **Nigeria's** new constitution, the president may declare an emergency in a state and suspend its government for a period, which has happened once. In **Russia**, the president has broad powers to declare a state of emergency in a part of the country and to suspend acts by the federal units that contravene the constitution, federal law, treaties, or the rights and freedoms of the human being. **Argentina** has seen over 175 federal interventions in provincial affairs, including the removal of governments, but the courts have declined to rule on this matter, which they deem to be political. **Pakistan's** federal government can name provincial governors, approve the dissolution of a provincial assembly by the governor, appoint caretaker provincial governments, and provide directions to a province. The **South African** constitution permits the central government to issue directives to a province or directly assume a provincial responsibility when the province is in breach of its legal or constitutional obligations; but to be continued, such actions are submitted to the upper house and require its approval and periodic review.

Constitutional amendment

Federal constitutions have special procedures and majorities for their amendment, often requiring some measure of consent by the legislatures or populations of constituent units. Consequently, constitutions can be difficult to amend and alternatives to formal constitutional change are frequently sought to adapt federations to changing circumstances.

Democracies usually have special procedures and majorities for constitutional amendment. This is particularly true in federations, where the federal principle leads to a role for constituent units in constitutional amendment, especially in coming-together federations as opposed to formerly unitary federations. Federations often give constituent units an absolute veto over certain matters affecting them directly, notably changes in their boundaries or merger with another unit. Federations vary greatly in how much consent is necessary to change the powers of all constituent units: this can range from not much more than a majority to virtual unanimity.

Consent for constitutional amendments usually involves legislatures and executives, but there can also be a requirement for a majority or special majority in a referendum vote. As well, constituent units may have a smaller or no role in relation to amendments that do not affect them directly. Constituent units are usually free to amend their own constitutions, where changes are within the permitted bounds of the federal constitution.

Amendment rules have often made constitutions difficult to change and the politics of constitutional amendment can prove very divisive. As a consequence, federations frequently look for alternatives to constitutional amendment.

Constitutional Amendment in Some Federations

The **United States** Constitution requires approval of two-thirds of members in both national houses and of three-quarters of states. **Brazil** requires 60 per cent in both houses, but, given the dominance of senators from small states, this is a high threshold. **Spain** requires special majorities within the two houses but no role for the autonomous communities. **Austria** normally requires only a special majority in the lower house or a national majority in a referendum. **Belgium**, though not centralized, has an elaborate procedure culminating in a need for a two-thirds majority in both houses (thus in effect requiring substantial consent from both major communities). **Russia** normally requires supermajorities in both houses and two-thirds of subjects of the federation. **South Africa** requires special majorities in the lower house plus the consent of six of the nine provinces for amendments affecting them. **Australia** requires double majorities of those voting in a national referendum on changes to the federal constitution: a national majority plus majorities in four of the six states.

Some federations have different amendment rules for different sections of their constitution: thus **Canada** has at least five rules, with some issues requiring unanimous consent. Likewise **India** has different rules for different sections: the unusual non-involvement of states in changes to state boundaries was deliberately chosen in the expectation that early adjustments to state boundaries would have to be made.

Rights in federal constitutions

Many federal constitutions have provisions relating to rights that can be invoked in relation to laws or actions of governments. Rights can be political, legal, social, linguistic, or economic. They can be important as political symbols. They can apply equally throughout the federation or be specific to a constituent unit or a population. The interpretation of rights is a central role for courts in many federations.

While federations are based on an allocation of powers to the two orders of government, these powers are typically constrained by provisions regarding rights that are set out in a constitution. Thus legislative authority over criminal law may be constrained by various legal rights, while that over education may be constrained by the constitutional right of certain populations to education or schools in their own language or religion. Such constitutional entrenchment of rights can be an important part of a federal deal or agreement because it provides certain protections when powers are transferred to the central government or to constituent-unit governments when the federation is created.

Protections for minority rights can be especially important in this regard. Constitutions are major symbols in defining a country, and rights provisions can be particularly important with the public. Minority rights provisions in particular can be a source of pride and unity or of discord within a country. Many rights provisions apply equally to all orders of government in a federation, but others, notably minority rights, might be quite different in different jurisdictions. As well, some constituent units have their own constitutions with rights provisions that may differ from those in the national constitution.

There is tremendous variety in the kinds of rights written into constitutions as well as the way they are expressed. The classic rights are political (freedom of speech, assembly, press, and religion) and legal (protection against arbitrary arrest and detention, due process of law). They may be economic (property). Some federal constitutions also entrench particular rights regarding specified languages or religions (language of government, denominational schools). Some constitutions also protect equality rights (against discrimination on whatever basis). Some have ambitious statements of economic and social rights (to employment, schooling), which may be viewed more as goals than enforceable rights because of the limited means of government, especially in poor countries. Brazil has many highly specific rights, such as no seizure of rural family property for debt or the right to higher pay for night shifts. A few federations have constitutionalized special rights of aboriginal or indigenous populations. Bosnia-Herzegovina's constitution incorporates international human rights instruments into domestic law.

Court interpretations of rights provisions can have very broad implications for the functioning of a federation. Older constitutions usually have more concise and classic lists of rights, while newer constitutions (or those recently amended) have longer lists that cover not just classic rights but also various rights important to key groups.

Role and character of the courts

Given the importance of judicial interpretation of the constitution, the legitimacy of the courts is a key issue. It will be affected by how judges are named and the role courts assume. There are frequent debates about the appropriate role for the judiciary because judges are not accountable to the population. Judicial procedures for dispute resolution need to be balanced by political procedures as well.

Most federations have procedures for ensuring that candidates for judgeships (especially high courts) are screened for professional competence. Some, notably presidential regimes, require judicial nominations to be reviewed by at least one house of the legislature. Some consult the constituent units on such nominations and even require their consent. In a number of federations, there is a formal or informal allocation of places on the high court to judges from specified constituent units, languages, or legal backgrounds (where the country has more than one judicial system). Finally, judicial independence is normally protected by strong tenure—making it very difficult to remove a judge during his or her term. Good salaries can make judges less susceptible to bribes.

There is always some dimension of political choice in naming judges, so that the balance of a court can be influenced by the political views and preferences of those selecting the judges. Alternation of parties in government tends to produce more balanced courts, as do procedures to ensure high professional competence. No high court is immune from charges of bias, so it is important that it have a stock of credibility and legitimacy when dealing with controversial cases. While some federations are very successful in this, in others, the independence or competence of the courts is regarded as weak—even as heavily influenced by the executive or susceptible to bribes.

However courts are established, a judicial system can be stressed in dealing with very divisive cases. The political fights over abortion and civil rights in the United States have both played out heavily through the courts. In India, frustrated citizens are making increasing appeals to the courts on issues such as air pollution and the monkey population in Delhi, issues that involve as much policy as legal content. Sometimes a court can make costly rulings on such issues without having the responsibility to implement them.

In some federations, the courts' role on certain matters is limited because disputes are assigned to another body (e.g., the water commission in India), or major agreements are political, not legal (e.g., federal-provincial agreements in Canada), or governments are required to solve disputes, even over the constitution, through political procedures before recourse to the courts (e.g., South Africa).

Chapter Eight

Intergovernmental Relations and Politics

Interdependence and interaction

All federations have considerable interdependence between governments. How politicians, civil servants, citizens, and other stakeholders try to influence outcomes in jurisdictions other than their own goes to the heart of each federation's political life.

Interdependence is inevitable and significant in all federations. It is particularly marked in federations where the constituent-unit governments deliver many federally legislated programs or laws, where there is extensive concurrency or joint responsibility in many areas, and where the constituent units depend heavily on conditional financing from the central government.

Federations can deal with this interdependence through formal, even constitutionalized, mechanisms, or ad hoc and informal arrangements. Heads of governments and ministers can dominate, or legislatures can play an important role. Political parties can be important. There can be highly differing levels of consultation, coordination, and cooperation, and this will vary, not only between federations and subjects, but also between controversial policy issues and more routine administration. All federations have some measure of cooperation and conflict. On controversial issues, the central government can try to influence constituent governments through its financial or legal powers, while the latter may withhold their consent if that is legally possible. Both can try to win public support to advance their goals.

Roles of executive and legislative branches

Strong executive branches lead to a focus on executive federalism in intergovernmental relations, while weaker executive branches lead to a greater role for legislatures. While parliamentary regimes usually have stronger executives than presidential-congressional regimes, there is no firm rule. The role and strength of executives or legislatures can change significantly, even without institutions being formally modified, especially because of changes in the political party regime.

In modern federations, the executive branch is typically dominant relative to the legislative branch of government. This is often true in parliamentary regimes because parties need discipline and the support of the legislature to form a government. But governments within parliamentary regimes can be weak because they lack a stable majority or consist of a loose coalition. Presidential-congressional regimes have a division of powers between the executive and legislative branches and this can lead to a diffusion of power, with the legislature playing an independent role and being engaged directly in relations with constituent governments (which lobby the members of the legislature). But some presidential regimes have strong executives, especially when the presidential party is disciplined and in control of the congress. As well, in some cases, such as Argentina, the Presidency has important quasi-legislative powers to issue decrees.

The party regime is critical. In federations where the political parties are integrated between the two orders of government, the national party leaders may have great influence over candidates and leaders in the constituent units; alternatively, regional barons, with their power bases in the constituent units, may be king makers for the party at the centre. India and Mexico both once had a single dominant party with strong central control and both have evolved to a multi-party regime with more decentralized parties (even though India is parliamentary and Mexico presidential-congressional) and a weakened executive. South Africa and Ethiopia each have one centralized party that effectively dominates constituent-unit politics. German parties at both levels are closely linked because of the role of *Länder* in the central government and many important intergovernmental issues are worked out within their parties as well as between their governments. Even in federations with very integrated party systems, politicians at one level have different constituencies and interests from those of party colleagues at the other level: some of these differences may be resolved within the party, others within intergovernmental forums.

Canada and the United States are federations whose parties have weak links between the two levels. But Canadian parties at each level are quite disciplined and the executive branches strong, so it is perhaps the classic case of executive federalism between governments. American parties are much less disciplined and the executives are weaker, so intergovernmental relations largely play out in lobbying by state governments and in myriad individual lobbying efforts, with almost no structures of executive federalism.

Upper houses in intergovernmental relations

Upper houses have often been seen as federal houses, in that their composition in some way reflects regional factors. In practice, few are important in intergovernmental relations. However, they can influence the relative weight of constituent units within central institutions, especially when the upper house has significant powers and its composition favours small constituent units.

In Germany, the upper house is formed of representatives of constituent-unit governments. The Bundesrat formally brings executive federalism into the legislative process, with representatives of *Länder* governments voting on issues directly affecting them. South Africa has largely adopted this model with the provincial governments being represented in the National Council of the Provinces, but its role has so far been limited because of the African National Congress's control of all governments.

Upper houses that are indirectly elected (by constituent-unit legislatures) typically play a relatively minor role in intergovernmental relations (as opposed to other matters) because they send representatives of both government and opposition parties (though the former will usually represent their government's views). Where members of the upper house are elected directly by the population, they tend to vote more along party than regional lines and to be quite independent of their constituent-unit governments. Of course, sometimes, party leaders at one level can influence the election of certain candidates at the other level, and then use them to pursue intergovernmental goals. As well, some government leaders have patronage powers that can influence members of another legislature. Even so, most upper houses play a limited role in intergovernmental relations as such. Where they may have a greater federal impact is in federations that give small constituent units equal representation or disproportionate weight in the upper house, and the upper house has significant powers. This situation can favour smaller units in central decision making.

Institutions and processes

Federations use various institutions and processes for intergovernmental relations. These can be formal or even constitutional, but often they are informal. Most federations manage intergovernmental relations through many kinds of political and legal instruments.

The main focus of intergovernmental relations is always vertical relations between the central government and the constituent units. Horizontal relations between constituent units tend to be less important and developed, with the focus often on regional cooperation between some constituent units. In some federations (Switzerland, Canada), the constituent units have mechanisms to promote the development of common positions in dealing with the central government, but this can be difficult where interests diverge.

Most federations are characterized by a dense network of relationships between governments: between heads of government, ministers, other elected officials, senior civil servants, policy advisors, and local administrators. At the highest level, in most central and constituent-unit governments, both the head of government and certain key ministers are deeply involved.

- Heads of government usually have an office for intergovernmental relations close to them (in the cabinet office or interior ministry, often with a responsible minister). Many federations have regular meetings between heads of government, which can be useful in resolving issues and developing relationships.

• Finance ministers always play a major role in fiscal federalism and other economic issues. Their ministries usually have a special staff for this function. Frequently, links between finance officials are highly developed.

• Other ministers, at both levels, will be engaged depending on their interests.

The United States is exceptional in having no structured system of executive federalism, notably amongst chief executives. Other presidential-congressional regimes in Latin America and in Nigeria typically have some structured arrangements.

Top politicians tend to lead on the major issues. For their meetings to succeed, it is important that they be well prepared and that their decisions be followed up. So, below them, there are all kinds of relationships: sometimes to work out details of a policy, sometimes to deal with administration. The mechanisms in support of such relationships cover the full range of organizational, legal, and political possibilities. A few federations have adopted organizational innovations that attract international attention. For example, Australia has an independent grants commission with a large staff charged with assessing the fiscal capacity and needs of states and making recommendations on grants; a loans council for approving state loans; and the Council of Australian Governments, which brings together First Ministers and other ministers with the assistance of a secretariat. The Swiss cantons have created a cantonal council to deal with issues between themselves, but also to coordinate their positions with the central government. However, experience suggests that the success of any standing institutions of this type is highly dependent on the context of politics and issues in which they operate.

Coercive versus consultative federalism

In some federations, the central government is quite dominant and can be coercive in relations with the constituent units. In others, there is more equality and a greater emphasis on consultation and negotiated agreements. While all federations combine some measure of cooperation and conflict between governments, the political climate of intergovernmental relations in federations differs greatly.

In some federations, the central government has strong legislative powers (such as concurrency) over the constituent units or a strong spending power, so it can be quite unilateral legislatively, or use conditional grants to induce constituent units to comply. Constituent units may try to use intergovernmental relations to limit these powers, but their success will depend on their ability to rally political support. The United States has many features of coercive federalism, and, given the relative absence of intergovernmental institutions, states rely heavily on lobbying within Congress to promote their interests. Some very highly centralized federations, such as Malaysia, have little structured intergovernmental dialogue because the constituent units are so weak.

In other federations, the central government is more constrained and must adopt a consultative and cooperative approach. Usually this reflects important political assets of the constituent-unit governments (powers, patronage, finances) and perhaps strong regional cleavages in the country (Canada, India). In some cases (Germany, Switzerland, South Africa), there is a culture of cooperation, which may even be a constitutional principle, though Germany shows how such a culture can be frayed by partisan conflict. Canada, Australia, India, Mexico, and Brazil tend to have quite conflictual politics, rooted in the functioning of their institutions and characteristics of their societies, but in all cases there are issues where both orders of government see a common interest in reaching agreement.

Chapter Nine

Unity and Diversity

Challenge of unity

Unity is a key issue or challenge in many federations, particularly those with major divisions of identity along class, linguistic, ethnic, religious, and other lines. A major unity challenge can exist in both federal and non-federal regimes. In some cases, the challenge takes the form of a separatist movement.

We have seen that federations are extremely varied in their institutions and social make-up.

- Some are relatively **homogenous** and citizens share a strong and dominant sense of a national identity. In these federations, unity is not a major issue and the social forces in the federation often create pressures for further centralization.

- Others are very **diverse** and citizens identify with very distinct groups, which have conflicting views or objectives. In some cases, members of a particular group may see their identity as incompatible with the national identity, thus creating tensions around the issue of national unity. This is especially true where such a distinct population is regionally concentrated.

The Irish movement for Home Rule in nineteenth-century Britain, the long civil war in South Sudan, the Basque insurgency under Franco in Spain, and the current insurgency of Tamil rebels in Sri Lanka are all examples of major unity challenges in unitary countries. The United States, Nigeria, and Pakistan during their civil wars, and Canada, faced with a separatist movement in Quebec, are all examples of federations facing unity challenges. While the risk of separatism is often associated with federalism, historically, separatist movements have been prevalent in many unitary countries as well.

Repressing diversity

Major unity challenges can be met with repression, exclusion, and assimilationist policies, but these often worsen the problem and risk leading to violence.

Some governments, especially undemocratic ones, respond to challenges to unity by trying to assimilate distinct sub-populations into the mainstream or to repress their political liberties. While, historically, some assimilationist policies have succeeded in integrating a minority into the larger population (e.g., in adopting the majority language) such policies risk creating strong resentments and a sense of alienation. Some groups, notably immigrants, may accept assimilationist policies, e.g., into a majority language, which would be resisted by long-established groups within a country. If a group targeted by repressive policies becomes deeply alienated and sees little prospect of peaceful resolution, it can turn to violence.

Embracing diversity

Democracies, including federations, facing a unity challenge can promote a positive political nationality that citizens feel is compatible with their other important identities within a climate of tolerance and accommodation. Embracing diversity as a national value can enhance unity.

The long-term unity of a democracy requires that a substantial majority of its citizens have a sense of national identity and attachment to the country. This is least likely when an important group within the population believes that the national identity conflicts with its strongly felt regional, ethnic, religious, or linguistic identity—for example, because the population is seriously under-represented in government, its religion is discriminated against, or its language is not respected or permitted to be used.

Frequently the challenge of unity involves not only addressing the concerns of minority groups, but also promoting a political culture of tolerance and accommodation within the minority and majority communities. Some majorities have defined their country in terms that reflect only themselves, to the exclusion of minority communities. At a minimum, a more positive culture promotes tolerance and accommodation of differences, but it will be even more effective if there is a collective embrace of diversity as part of the national character, with symbols and policies that resonate with the different streams in the society. India, Nigeria, Ethiopia, Canada, Switzerland, and South Africa are all examples of federations whose approach to promoting unity involves the embrace of diversity.

Success in developing such a culture can be difficult if politicians or leaders within various communities (majority and minority) try to stir up strongly hostile feelings and fears between groups. A dominant majority, such as a religious or linguistic group, may be reluctant to give up its historic privileges. Yugoslavia is a tragic example. Positive leadership can be vital, as the examples of Mandela, Gandhi, and Nehru show.

A balanced approach to diversity

The embrace of diversity requires a balanced approach of 'building out' and 'building in'. Building out involves accommodating the demand for regional government. Building in involves ensuring that key minorities are integrated into the symbols, institutions, and policies of the central government as well as through other constitutional provisions.

Creating or strengthening regional governments controlled by local populations can empower a regional population to make decisions that are important to it. It also permits such populations to see their particular character reflected in local governmental institutions. These are central characteristics of a federal accommodation and culture that permits national and regional political communities to coexist in harmony.

At the same time, a policy of empowering constituent governments to the exclusion of accommodating key regional minorities within central institutions risks accelerating the dynamic of disintegration in a country. If key identity groups do not see themselves properly reflected in central institutions, there is little likelihood they will maintain or increase their sense of national identity and more likelihood that they will support ever more devolution—or secession.

Building out: devolution

Building out involves creating or empowering regionally defined constituent units to respond to the demands of a territorially concentrated population, and is at the heart of federal arrangements. However, there are practical issues: within an established federation, it can be difficult to create new units; regional boundaries rarely enclose a very homogenous population, so there can be significant minorities within regions; there may be a limit to how many regional units can realistically be created; some populations with a strong sense of distinct identity may be geographically dispersed; and strongly asymmetric arrangements can be hard to sustain.

The stability of many federations, notably very diverse ones, such as India, Canada, and Switzerland has depended on their devolved, federal form of government. However, once a federation takes shape, constitutional rules can make it difficult to redraw boundaries to create new constituent units. India is the most notable exception: it has redrawn the map of its states and periodically creates new states. Switzerland created the new canton of Jura after an elaborate referendum procedure. Nigeria's state boundaries were dramatically redrawn by military regimes using non-constitutional procedures.

As well, some federations, such as India, Nigeria, and Ethiopia, have far more language groups and ethnicities than they have constituent units: it is not practical to imagine that all small groups can have their own constituent unit (though some Indian states have sub-units within constituent units that have distinct majority populations.) Furthermore, populations do not live in tidy geographic parcels, so even constituent units that are home to a distinct population may not contain all of that population in the country; as well, they usually have one or more significant minorities within their constituent unit. Finally, some quite distinct ethnic, linguistic, or religious groups may be so widely dispersed that there is no prospect of their being the largest population within a constituent unit. Thus, the creation of constituent units can be part of a response to diversity, but it cannot be the whole answer.

In some cases, one part of a federation favours much more devolution than the other parts, which raises the possibility of asymmetric arrangements. However, these can be difficult to sustain if they entail significantly different constitutional powers for constituent units, especially when the unit receiving special powers is relatively large.

Building in: a representative centre

Building in promotes unity by enhancing the recognition and role of key populations within the institutions of the central government and by providing protection for minorities.

A balanced approach to a unity challenge normally includes measures for building in, to ensure that a key population with a distinct identity feels properly recognized and represented in the country's central institutions and broader constitutional provisions.

A balanced approach could include

- **defining the country or national community** with both nationally accepted symbols (rights, flag, etc.) and appropriate inclusion of the symbols, history, religion, and language of key populations (and not defining the country in terms of the majority population only);

- **promoting certain national programs** (e.g., a common market, a national health system, a national pension scheme) that are widely viewed as uniting, national projects of mutual benefit;

- **ensuring that key populations are properly represented and empowered in central institutions**: formal or informal practices can ensure a representative composition of the government, the civil service, the military; in extreme cases, (e.g., post-conflict) there may be negotiated power sharing within the government between the key communities;

- protecting minorities within the constituent units: federations often have different majorities and minorities at the national and constituent-unit level; protecting minorities within the units (language, religion, school rights, civil service, etc.) can be part of a balance of rights and protections in the whole federation.

Language policy is often very sensitive. One of the great advantages of federalism in linguistically diverse countries is that it permits different languages to predominate in different areas (building out), but it must also address the language concerns of minorities at the national and constituent-unit levels (building in). In practice, language policy is often highly complex with many special arrangements. In some federations (India, Nigeria, Malaysia, Ethiopia), in addition to provision for local languages, a non-indigenous language might be adopted as a major link language because it is seen as more neutral (English, for example, also has the advantage of being a major international language). Pakistan has adopted Urdu, the language of a small minority, as the official language, though English and Punjabi remain very important; and Indonesia, which is not a federation, also chose to make a small minority language the official language, Indonesian.

Majorities can be resentful of the need to accommodate minority languages, just as minorities can be insistent on accommodation. Each country must find its own equilibrium. Often (Canada, India, Switzerland, Ethiopia), some language rights at both the central and constituent-unit levels are protected in the federal constitution. In other cases, such rights are primarily matters of law or practice and are left to each order of government. The philosophy underlying language policies differs across federations: some emphasize the rights of individuals wherever they are; others tie language rights to particular locations (or to tiers of government).

Aspects of Language Policy in Some Federations

India has 40 languages with more than one million speakers and 18 constitutional languages: Hindi (mother tongue of 18 per cent and spoken by over 40 per cent) is the leading indigenous language; English is important as a link language. States may choose which constitutional language is official and provide services in official or other languages. **Nigeria** has three important indigenous languages that are official, but at least 450 others; English is the principal language of government and education, though local languages can be used; some rights of citizens, e.g., in the courts, are based on a language that is understood, not preferred. **Ethiopia** has two major indigenous languages, as well as 11 minor and many tribal ones: there is no official language and all enjoy equal recognition in principle. English is also used in education and government. Amarhic is the working language of the federal government and of some state governments; each state chooses its language(s) of work. **South Africa** has two European languages and nine significant indigenous languages, no one of which is spoken by more than a quarter of the population. English is the dominant language, though local languages are encouraged for oral use in the local administration and in some teaching. In **Malaysia**, Malay is the mother tongue of 62 per cent of the population and is the official language, though English is prominent as a language of use in government and the courts; minority language rights are very limited. **Switzerland** has three official languages and one national language at the federal level, with 19 unilingual and three bilingual cantons and one trilingual canton: in unilingual cantons, all public services and education are in the local language only. **Belgium**, too, emphasizes territorial language rights, with the Dutch-and French-speaking communities and regions providing services in their language only; Brussels and the federal government are bilingual. **Canada** is officially bilingual federally and in New Brunswick, with other provinces providing various rights for minorities: rights to federal services in the language of choice exist 'where numbers warrant'. Canadian law includes language requirements for labeling packages sold in commerce. In **Spain**, Castilian is the unique national language that 'all Spaniards have the duty to know and use'; it is the mother tongue of three-quarters of the population. There are seven languages of 'nationalities', the largest of which, Catalan, is the first language of 60 per cent of Catalans. Catalan, Basque, Galician, and Valencian are the only languages of 'nationalities' that can be co-official with Spanish in their respective autonomous communities, with varying rights and duties.

Unity post-conflict

Creating unity in post-conflict environments poses special challenges. Federalism may be part of a peace plan or strategy.

Most long-established federations emerged peacefully. Switzerland is something of an exception: it became a federation after a brief conflict amongst cantons of the previous confederation. A number of federations have experienced periods of internal violence: the civil wars over secession in the United States and Nigeria; the Mexican revolution; various Argentine conflicts; insurgency in Spain's Basque country. Societies are usually deeply divided after such conflicts and it can take a long time for politics to normalize, but, in all the countries mentioned, the issue of secession is either resolved or much reduced.

In recent years, there have been various experiments introducing federal arrangements as part of peace plans after conflicts: Bosnia-Herzegovina, Sudan, the Democratic Republic of the Congo, and Iraq have all adopted federal institutions or committed to them, but the implementation has been difficult and the situations remain fragile. Federalism is currently being considered in Nepal after the end of a Maoist insurgency and as a possible solution to the conflict in Sri Lanka. While there is logic to federal arrangements in such cases, the challenge is to achieve the level of trust or mutual accommodation needed to permit political institutions to function with some degree of stability.

The question of secession

There is no standard constitutional approach to dealing with the possibility of secession. Many federal constitutions exclude the possibility, but there are exceptions. Developing democratic procedures for secession poses significant issues.

Many federations have constitutional provisions asserting the eternal unity of the country or precluding the possibility of secession. The United States (an 'indestructible union'), Mexico, Brazil, Nigeria, India, and Spain are examples. (Spain also prohibits autonomous communities from holding referendums on secession.) In other cases, such as Australia, Germany, and Switzerland, the constitution is silent on the issue. Ethiopia's constitution is unusual in providing a formal right to secession, though this remains controversial and untested. Sudan provides for the possibility of a referendum on the independence of Southern Sudan after the ten-year, interim period of the peace agreement, during which there are power-sharing and federal arrangements.

International law sees the right of secession as legitimate only in cases of severe abuse of the human rights of a population and of decolonization. The international community is normally hostile to secession because it can destabilize international relations. In Africa, where political boundaries cut across so many ethnicities, a right to secession could undermine the whole state structure of the continent. Despite this, there have been cases of secession or dissolution of countries in recent decades, including the USSR, Yugoslavia, Czechoslovakia, Pakistan, and Malaysia (actually the expulsion of Singapore).

The right to secession poses a dilemma for democratic federations. Such a right can lead to its own tensions in that it questions the solidarity of the national community and can risk regional blackmail. Federations are based on the notion that citizens belong both to the national and to their regional (constituent-unit) communities. Over time, many decisions, commitments, and compromises can be made that give all parts of the country a moral investment in its continuance. Against this, a clear majority in favour of secession poses a critical issue for a federation. Canada's Supreme Court ruled that, in a province, a clear majority voting on a clear question in favour of secession would give the province a right to pursue secession through negotiations, with no conclusions predetermined by law. The negotiations would need to reconcile the rights of two legitimate majorities and their ultimate conclusion would be political. Thus the court found something less than a right to secede, but gave moral weight to a clear vote for secession. In 2006, Montenegro seceded from Yugoslavia, having met the threshold of a 55 per cent vote in favour, which had been agreed to in advance.

Chapter Ten

Thinking About Federalism

Federalism's strengths and limits

Federalism has an important place in the world's tool kit for democratic governance. It has proven itself in a number of long-established and prosperous democracies. However, federalism cannot guarantee democracy or good governance any more than unitary government can.

While federalism is clearly a proven form of governance, it has many of the strengths and weaknesses of other forms of democratic governance. Federalism is not immune to conflict, corruption, or the breakdown of democratic order. However, it is clearly appropriate to the circumstances of many countries, notably democracies with large populations or large territories or very diverse populations. A number of long-established federations, such as the US and Australia, have become more centralized because of modern communications, a drive for coordinated policies, and the pressure of globalization, but others, such as Canada, India, and Switzerland have remained or become quite decentralized.

Federalism's growing relevance

Increased attention to federalism is being driven by the spread of democratic government, by the growth of identity politics in some countries, by new experiments in bringing formerly sovereign countries together, and by attempts to find stable governance formulas in post-conflict situations.

A whole series of factors are making federalism more relevant in the modern world. Perhaps most fundamental is the spread of democratization, which is bringing life to some previously authoritarian federations, or creating pressures for federalism in some previously unitary regimes. As well, federalism is being turned to in post-conflict situations where there are strong internal or external forces against secession.

Conditions for federal success

Federalism works best where there is broad respect for the rule of law, a culture of tolerance and accommodation between population groups, and significant elements of shared identity. Institutional arrangements can be important in achieving stability.

While some federations have survived deep trauma, there is no doubt that a federation functions best in a society that respects the rule of law and independence of the courts. In highly diverse societies, it requires a political culture of tolerance and accommodation. In federations with deep regional cleavages along ethnic, linguistic, or religious lines, stability can be enhanced if the culture goes beyond mere tolerance of diversity to the active embrace of diversity as part of what defines the country and gives its value. Institutional arrangements can help societies manage their conflicts, but institutions alone are not enough: there must be a broader commitment in the society to a spirit of diversity.

Leaders can be important in this regard: do they divide the society, as Milosevic did in Yugoslavia, or do they build a spirit of national sharing, as Gandhi and Nehru did in India, and Mandela in South Africa?

Various past federal experiments failed, but these were typically in cases with immature democracies, little history of a shared country, or a federal structure of only two or three constituent units, each representing very distinct communities. In some highly diverse countries, federalism may be the only form of constitutional government that would be consistent with democratic stability.

Learning from comparative federalism

There are no easy formulas for designing or understanding federal institutions. But comparative knowledge of various federations can help in considering how different federal arrangements might play out in a particular context.

The politics of complex societies does not permit simplistic 'cookbook' approaches to institutional design. We have seen that similar institutions can operate quite differently in various political or social contexts. The same federal arrangements will play out very differently if grafted onto a more homogenous versus a more diverse society. As well, often the devil is in the details, so that we must look beyond the major institutional arrangements—the number of units, the division of powers, the executive and legislative structures—to understand the more detailed rules and practices that may have grown up to shape their actual functioning. The study of comparative federalism can provide us with a better sense of the questions to ask, of the connections to look out for, of likely impacts of certain arrangements. It makes us better observers and sharpens our judgment.

Acknowledgements

This book could never have been written without the benefit of key works on federalism. Foremost is Ron Watts's *Comparing Federal Systems*, which was a primary source for many of the comparative summaries and boxes. Ron, my former teacher and a founding director of the Forum of Federations, also reviewed the text, picking up numerous points, and generously shared the results of research on current fiscal arrangements in federations that he has gathered as he prepares the third edition of his classic book. I also benefited greatly from the work of the Forum of Federations' Global Dialogue program, which has now produced four significant volumes as well as six booklets. Other key sources are indicated in the suggestions for further reading.

The draft text was read by a number of scholarly friends, who made valuable comments: Miguel Angel Cabellos, David Cameron, Harvey Lazar, Peter Leslie, Richard Simeon, and Marie-Joelle Zahar. Forum staff members Raoul Blindenbacher, Celine Auclair, Rupak Chattopadyhay, and Rod Macdonell all contributed comments and other assistance. Ernest Hillen and Marta Tomins did a superb job of editing, and Marta provided an invaluable introduction to David Stover at Oxford University Press Canada. Yash Ghai and Jill Cottrell in Kathmandu showed early enthusiasm in having a rough first draft translated into Nepali. My wife, Charlotte Gray, provided the model for clear prose. . . and so much more.

Further Readings

There is a vast literature on federalism. The following selections focus on relatively recent publications with a comparative perspective.

Ugo M.Amoretti and Nancy Bermeo, eds. *Federalism and Territorial Cleavages* (Johns Hopkins University Press: Baltimore, 2004)

Richard Bird and Thomas Stauffer, eds., *Intergovernmental Fiscal Relations in Fragmented Societies* (Institute of Federalism: Fribourg, Switzerland, 2001)

Raoul Blindenbacher and Arnold Koller, eds., *Federalism in a Changing World: Learning from Each Other* (McGill-Queen's University Press: Montreal, 2003)

Robin Boadway and Anwar Shah, eds., *Intergovernmental Fiscal Transfers: Principles and Practice* (World Bank: Washington, DC, 2007)

Michael Burgess, *Comparative Federalism: Theory and Practice* (Routledge: London, 2006)

D.J. Elazar, *Exploring Federalism* (University of Alabama Press: Tuscaloosa, 1987)

Edward L. Gibson, ed., *Federalism and Democracy in Latin America* (Johns Hopkins University Press: Baltimore, 2001)

Ann L. Griffiths, ed., *Handbook of Federal Countries, 2005* (McGill-Queen's for the Forum of Federations: Montreal, 2005)

Thomas O. Heuglin and Alan Fenna, *Comparative Federalism: A Systematic Inquiry* (Broadview Press: Peterborough Ontario, 2006)

International Social Science Journal, Special Issue on Federalism (2001)

John Kincaid and G. Alan Tarr, eds., *Constitutional Origins, Structure, and Change in Federal Countries,* (McGill-Queen's University Press: Montreal, 2005)*

Katy Le Roy and Cheryl Saunders, *Legislative, Executive and Judicial Governance in Federal Countries* (McGill-Queen's University Press: Montreal, 2006)*

Akhtar Majeed, Ronald L. Watts and Douglas M. Brown, *Distribution of Powers and Responsibilities in Federal Countries* (McGill-Queen's University Press: Montreal, 2006)*

Publius: The Journal of Federalism, Special Issue: The Global Review of Federalism (2002)

Anwar Shah, ed., *The Practice of Fiscal Federalism: Comparative Perspectives* (McGill-Queen's University Press: Montreal, 2007)*

G. Alan Tarr, Robert F. Williams, Josef Marko, eds., *Federalism, Subnational Constiutions, and Minority Rights* (Praeger: Westport, 2004)

Teresa Ter-Minassian, ed., *Fiscal Federalism in Theory and Practice* (International Monetary Fund: Washington, DC, 1997)

Ronald L. Watts, *Comparing Federal Systems,* 2ⁿᵈ edition (McGill-Queens University Press: Montreal, 1999). A third edition is expected in late 2007.

Ronald L. Watts, *The Spending Power in Federal Systems: A Comparative Study* (McGill-Queen's University Press: Montreal, 1999)

* Indicates a volume in the Forum of Federations and the International Association of Centres for Federal Studies, *A Global Dialogue on Federalism.* Volumes on *Foreign Relations in Federal Countries* (Hans J. Michelmann, ed.) and *Local Government and Metropolitan Regions in Federal Countries* (Nico Steytler, ed.) are in preparation and other subjects will follow. There are short booklets to accompany all of these volumes, published by the Forum of Federations and available on its website *www.forumfed.org. The website also includes many articles on federalism, including material from some of the volumes cited above*